D1795548

Sabine Lichtenfels • Dieter Duhm

AND THEY KNEW EACH OTHER

The End of Sexual Violence

Second edition, 2019 © Verlag Meiga GbR
ISBN 978-3-927266-62-9

Translated from the German by Sten Linnander, edited by Stephen Davis
Original title: *Und sie erkannten sich.*

Cover design and cover photo: Jörg Appenfelder, using vector graphics from https://freedesignfile.com, adapted by Lukas Mauermann

Photos in the book: Tamera Archive (if not stated otherwise)
Drawings and paintings by Dieter Duhm, art work by Sabine Lichtenfels

VERLAG MEIGA GBR
Waldsiedlung 15, D-14806 Bad Belzig, Germany.
Ph. +49-(0)33841-30538, Fax: -38550
Email: info@verlag-meiga.org
www.verlag-meiga.org

TABLE OF CONTENTS

INTRODUCTION TO THE ENGLISH EDITION

Dear Readers,

At the special request of some friends – especially from our network in the US – we asked Sabine Lichtenfels to summarize again the answer to why this book deals so explicitly with the relationship between man and woman. Here is her response:

"This book was written to end a millennium-old war: the war between the sexes, between the polar forces man and woman. It is a book for peace.

It is about raising awareness of a core injury that has taken place between the male and female forces. This violation is independent of the question of what sexual identity and preferences we choose in our personal life. These polar forces seek healing in each and every one of us. If you allow yourself to dive deeply into this book, you will realize that a newfound truth is revealed here that concerns everyone. If these poles no longer fight each other, but recognize each other, a central cause for war on Earth is eliminated.

With this in mind, we wholeheartedly invite everyone to participate in the peace work presented here, especially including those who can not or do not clearly associate themselves with the male or female gender, or who are attracted to same-sex partners. If this work succeeds, it will have a healing effect on all life. May this book become an inspiration to all who seek the truth in love and see the need to bring back the sacredness in Eros into life."

Sabine Lichtenfels

PREFACE BY THE PUBLISHERS

It was the midsummer 2016 when I first held the raw draft of this book in my hand. I was overwhelmed. What I read was, paragraph by paragraph, a new alphabet for our earthly existence; the cultural genetic code for a nonviolent civilization; a precious treasure, compiled by two pioneers in love, who had taken a stand for life.

This book leads us to those key points within, where the decision is made if life triumphs over fear, lies and hatred. It has the potential to trigger an unstoppable cultural and social revolution. Personally, I called it an "erotic manifesto," and I imagined it being read, studied and passed on all over the world.

What a challenge to collective intelligence to bring such a book into the world under the conditions of global capitalism! Anyone who wishes to contribute and cooperate is cordially invited to contact us.

To give the readers of this book the necessary breaks in this compact text, we have illustrated it with pictures. We used photos of the art work by Sabine Lichtenfels and especially drawings and paintings by Dieter Duhm with which he captured the joy of life sometimes in the form of quick sketches.

May the thoughts in this book contribute to empowering us to turn the Earth into a paradise – a paradise for all beings, both human and animal.

In the name of love,

Monika Berghoff

Acknowledgements by the Authors

We thank all the people who have participated in our work for forty years.

We thank all co-workers and guests who had the courage to uncover their inner motivations in life and thus became a model for others.

We thank those who dared get to the bottom of truth in the issues of sex, love and partnership. We thank the heavenly powers for the freedom that we needed to even be able to write this book.

We especially want to thank two women: Monika Berghoff and Leila Dregger. Their sensitivity and intelligence contributed significantly to the manifestation of this book.

In addition, we wish to thank the two men who made the wonderful cover: Lukas Mauermann and Jörg Appenfelder.

We give thanks for the deep lessons in love that we ourselves have had the opportunity to receive during our long work within community – and we are pleased to be able to pass on these teachings to others.

"And yet when reaching for the hand

Which would this light cup have bestowed,

The burden proved for both too great,

For both, in trembling, knew a state

Where neither hand its partner found,

And so to earth the dark wine flowed."

Excerpt from the poem „Die Beiden" ["The Two"]
by Hugo von Hofmannsthal

"Passing the Wine Glass," oil painting by Dieter Duhm, 1963

A Personal Foreword

We, the two authors of this book, have been living together for forty years. Perhaps we emerged, metaphorically speaking, from a single human primal cell. The cell then divided into two: one female and one male. The man developed a "male" line, the woman a "female" line. The two lines met forty years ago in Southern Germany and instinctively came together more deeply than they knew at the time. It was not even love at first sight, but rather a slow and continuous faithfulness that eventually passed even the most difficult of tests. What is it that brings a man and a woman together forever? Perhaps there is no more revealing issue than the inner connection between a male and a female source. The closer we became, the more we felt that we were dealing with an issue that had to do with the whole world. What happens between two lovers happens everywhere on Earth in one form or another. What we describe in this book is the generalization of an inner issue that we humans face when we – a man and a woman – no longer avoid the problems that have burdened the love between the sexes for generations. For nothing torments us more than despair in love and nothing is more beautiful than love fulfilled.

We have experienced both, but there were some things that kept bringing us together more and more: Our shared joy of sensual love – also with others – and the experience that this did not result in jealousy; then our shared commitment to the peace movement; and finally, our absolute faith in each other. In this unusual combination, we together decided to initiate a project for the healing of love.

There is a beautiful statement that says: "Heaven and Earth emerged from a primordial wedding night."

Would this not be a beautiful foundation for a new Creation Story? It would not begin with the fall of Adam and Eve, but with their love.

Independent of all gender issues of our times and independent of our momentary sexual identity, there is at the heart of human society the co-existence of the sexes. Their attraction or repulsion, their sexual signals and wiring, and their hopes and disillusionments run like a secret nervous system through all of human society. Man and woman – the two halves of human beings – long for each other, miss each other, fight each other and seek each other until they find each other. They must find each other, not only in pairs, but worldwide, for only then can the deepest wound of all be healed, the wound in love.

We ask for your understanding that we in this book focus so exclusively on the heterosexual relationship, for this is where the wound lies that is reproduced in all other forms of relationships. It is about the fundamental polarity of the male and female power. The relationship problems that we will deal with in this book also apply more or less to all forms of relationship, whether hetero- or homosexual. (More to this issue, see chapters 3 and 24.)

What happens out there in the world is a reflection of what happens inside of us. The problem lies between us human beings. Here, in our everyday life and our everyday relationships, especially in our love relationships, we find the issue around which the world revolves. To straighten out our own love life, we must step out of our private horizon and recognize that we are dealing with an issue affecting all of humanity. It is then no longer a question of individual therapy, but of establishing a humane culture. This was the key to the concrete utopia of global healing biotopes toward which we have been working for the past 40 years. The longer we work at it, the clearer we get an idea and a vision that has to do with love – love between humans, love of animals and love of God – in essence with the love between the sexes. This key issue was at the heart of our project right from the beginning. In this book we want to describe what we have found out in this regard during forty years of community experience.

We are writing this book as founders and spokespersons of the Tamera Project. Almost everybody who comes to us does so because of the issue of love. No matter what topics we present in our programs, people come with the hope of finding answers to their unsolved problems in the areas of love, sex and partnership. May this book contribute to the fulfillment of this hope.

Sabine Lichtenfels and Dieter Duhm

Tamera, 2018

PART I

Dieter Duhm

THE PRIMAL LOVE BETWEEN THE SEXES AND THE END OF SEXUAL VIOLENCE

1. COLLECTIVE MISERY IN LOVE: A GLOBAL ISSUE

We live in difficult times. Misery in love is part of the collective global "pain body." The relationship between the sexes constitutes one of the deepest war zones of our time. Here, many hopes have been dashed, many dreams have been shattered and many negative thoughts have arisen – thoughts of resignation, of irony, of revenge and violence. Only if we can create a social movement that provides a positive and convincing solution to this issue will we give our evolution a humane direction. Political and religious movements that cannot provide any answers in this regard will fail because of the overwhelming power of the opposing forces, which we also find within ourselves. They will fail because of the overwhelming power of their own unredeemed longings.

As long as the most intimate longings remain unfulfilled, the human being will always look for ideological, religious, professional or political substitute solutions; and the more they commit themselves to these substitute solutions, the more they will defend themselves against the revelation of inner truths. One does not want to touch the old wounds, the pain and the disappointments in love again. This path of avoidance and suppression keeps the wheel of the existing system turning – a system that permanently reproduces misery in love. This collective misery in love requires permanent compensation: consumption, addiction and violence.

Here we are formulating a connection between global war and the most intimate areas of human life. Do we seriously claim that liberating sexual and spiritual love is a prerequisite for global peace? We know that such statements may sound ideological to the ears of many of our contemporaries. Faced with the terrible events of our time, they cannot understand why we, who have for so long been politically involved, insist on focusing on inner topics with such passion. We do this because behind all external illusions there is hidden pain, hidden sadness or hidden anger that one no longer is willing to become aware of. We do this because, above all the clouds, there is still a brilliant sky, a world order of love – we call it the "sacred matrix."

Sexuality and love are gifts we receive from the universe. We have not created them; instead, they are part of the "other reality." All children are born from this reality. All peoples and all lovers are guided by the elementary powers of love and sexuality. The destiny of human beings depends on whether these powers are guided correctly or not. If they are guided correctly, they follow the path of healing, whereas if they are falsely guided, they follow the laws of conformism, repression, lies and violence.

In imperialist societies people hardly had a chance to develop their sexual powers of love freely, for the patriarchal world could only function by suppressing and controlling these forces. Whoever controls sexuality controls the entire human being. People were forced to hide their feelings and their erotic impulses and wear an exterior mask to avoid punishment. These circumstances brought a lie into the world that resulted in spiritual pain, violence and war. The elementary powers of life could no longer be realized in the form of a free, loving and humane existence. We need a different life order to liberate and heal these core energies. Ending the secret or open war between the sexes is a social issue – and ultimately an ecological, political and spiritual issue. The key words for establishing permanent joy in love are trust and community. These are also the key words for the success of the global transformation that wants to manifest today.

Society today focuses on technological progress: incredible things are being developed there. Artificial cells that can reproduce are created in high-tech laboratories. Robots are sent to comets billions of miles away, and now the first manned space mission to Mars is being prepared. These are, no doubt, great achievements. Old limitations are overcome on a fundamental level and a new code of what is possible emerges. But the technological developments are disastrous so long as they are not connected to the inner development of the human being. When people fly to Mars, they will simply export the old mentality of the war society to another planet. The misery in love will continue, both on Earth and on Mars. What if the same amount of intelligence and willpower that has thus far been invested in technical progress, were devoted to the human being's inner areas, to his spiritual development, his capacity for love, truth, and community, and to solidarity with all our fellow creatures? The invention of the steam engine, the use of oil, the discovery of nuclear fission and the development of electronic data processing have revolutionized the material world of human beings, often with terrible consequences.

Couldn't a global transformation towards love and solidarity occur, thereby changing the world more than anything else has so far?

Is there perhaps a blueprint of Creation (in the "implicate order" of the world), in which fear and violence simply do not exist? Today, we are approaching the realization that such a design actually exists. At its center we find the mystery of love. Religions have taught us that "God is love." But what God and what love? By exploring these questions, we come face to face with the deepest system change in the worldwide historical process that we today call "transformation."

To find the answers, we should not focus too quickly on the constantly burning issue of love and sexuality. We will recognize that to solve the issue we need to include other areas of life that we normally do not think about when dealing with sex and love. This includes all areas that deal with our co-existence with the beings and powers of nature – the ethics of dealing with all our co-creatures. In all areas of life, we find the same fundamental laws of a higher world order, which we call the "sacred matrix."

If we follow the basic rules of universal life, the ethics of compassion, love and support arise all on their own.

2. BEYOND ALL THE TEARS

What is happening on Earth today is too terrible, too viciously cruel to endure. The only thing that protects us is distance. If we could experience up close what people are doing to each other, what they have been doing to each other for thousands of years, and what is being repeated today on a global scale, we would be bereft of all hope: Syria, the bombs, the "Islamic State," the homeless children, the methods used by the corporations, governments and intelligence services. The spiral of power and destruction has reached a global culmination. The world is experiencing a global catastrophe. The current refugee issue is not just an issue for the refugees; it is a topic for humanity as a whole. Many co-workers at Tamera have been active in refugee assistance in Lesbos, Idomeni and other places. They have seen for themselves what is happening to the refugees. But they have also seen how many people came to help with open hearts. Many came to feed the hungry, provide shelter for the refugees, pull children from the flames, and – often risking their lives – provide information about the political background of globalized cruelty. But this cruelty could not be stopped.

If we consider everything, we only have two options: either we look away and give up, or we identify the causes of the collective drama and build another world.

As Etty Hillesum, a Dutch Jew, wrote in her diary just before her death in the concentration camp at Auschwitz: "The misery is truly great, and yet in the evenings, when the day has settled deep down within me, I walk along the barbed wire with light steps and then, over and over again, my heart overflows. I cannot help it, it just happens, it's an elementary power: Life is something wonderful and great. Later we must build a whole new world – and we need to meet every further crime and every further cruelty with a further bit of love and kindness that we must set free within ourselves."

3. WHY THE FOCUS ON MAN AND WOMAN?

The polarity of forces belongs to the spiritual order of the Universe. The mystery of erotic polarity is a fundamental reality of our cosmic existence. Masculine and feminine are the two creative archetypal poles in the soul of humanity. All of life, both physical and spiritual, originates from their union. Their polarity is a source of infinite happiness, creativity, insight and love whenever they can complement each other; yet if they don't, it leads to war, disease, fear and unhappiness..

I find it to be a miracle of existence that this fundamental polarity of our collective soul has also expressed itself in the physical polarity of men and women and their overwhelming longing to unite in flesh, heart and soul. It's as if the soul of the world would seek its unity through our longing for each other. I don't know any power on Earth that is greater than this desire. Whether this longing will continue to result in devastation or whether we will find the social intelligence to lead it to fulfillment, will be fundamental to whether or not we will survive the global crises we have provoked.

Let me be clear. My focus on man and woman in no way means to exclude non-heterosexual relationships and people with non-binary sexual identities or even demean them as inferior. I believe that no matter in which body or relationship we live, we all carry both masculine and feminine energies within us and are all seeking to find the place of union in polarity. Everyone who has the possibility to express themselves freely and truthfully in an environment of trust will chose the sexual identity and forms of relationship that they need for their healing and to take their specific role contributing to the whole of life. Yet life isn't just uniform but unfolds itself in ever growing diversity. Many Indigenous cultures that have been centered around guarding the balance between masculine and feminine powers acknowledged the existence of more than two genders and honored "two spirits," i.e. those who combine both male and female in one body, as people with particular proximity to the sacred. I mention this to highlight that no external moral law must prescribe to others what their "right" sexual identity and expression should look like. There is only the authentic human experience and the freedom to follow it. Wherever and however this happens authentically, it is a contribution to the healing of love and sexuality. To find our way we need to be open to all paths and eliminate all factors that force us to lie.

And here lies the crucial point. Truth in love and sexuality has hardly been possible during the past millennia of patriarchal rule, and least so between men and women. I'm focusing so deliberately on the heterosexual relationship because here is where the patriarchal wound originated and is constantly perpetuated. Having been caught in a pattern of victim and perpetrator, attack and defense, fear and disguise, men and women have not come together. The result was an epochal nightmare for children who, when they grew up, passed the suffering they had endured on to the next generation. There were doubtless many reasons for the global escalation of violence, but at its core there was – and still is today – the drama of the genders. Ending this drama is the task of a global peace movement. Nowadays, many people are trying to free themselves from this misery by breaking out of the old patriarchal gender roles. This is certainly a step in the right direction; yet for the patriarchal wound to actually heal, it is essential to rediscover the original love between men and women, behind all distortion and abuses of history. We can develop the most beautiful ideas for humane renewal – humane ecology, technology, economy, legislation or religion – but as long as this core issue has not been solved, life on Earth cannot heal. The genetic code of a humane new world – indeed, the genetic code of the new planet Earth – contains a new relationship between the genders.

This original love is one of greatest gifts we have received from the Universe. Here, a primal spark of an overwhelming vitality is ignited. A key to turn from war to peace lies in a deep understanding between the genders and a grateful affirmation of their spiritual and sensual appreciation of each other. Woman is spiritual and physical love incarnate, and man will always seek her, for she is his holy grail. This world is not meant to be a battlefield but a love affair.

People's inner lives are characterized by dreams, longings and images that are etched into the sacred matrix of love as archetypal primal forces. If we follow the spiritual history of love between the genders back to its origin, we find two archetypal images: the archetypal image of the positive father and the archetypal image of the positive mother.

Children are born between the great thighs of a woman. We all had our first home inside the body of a woman. The embodiment of home is feminine. This is independent of our current sexual identity. We all carry this memory of our origins as an unconscious collective image in our souls. The Goddess images of the "Great Mother," the worship of Mary, the entire iconography of humanity is full of this primary fact of our human existence.

The tension resulting from the dichotomy between those two archetypal images can easily lead to conflict and war if it is permeated by fear and distrust. Today, we are slowly emerging from a history that was obsessed by the magic of sexual polarity without being able to integrate it into social life. From the Grimm brother's fairy tales to Hollywood there is a recurrent theme of love through all the stories, but the world was not organized so that the love that was so coveted could find permanence. It was compressed into a much too narrow concept of faithfulness, partnership and marriage so that the deeper meaning of partnership and marriage was lost. Until now there has hardly been any true and permanent partnership that could fully integrate vibrant Eros. Historically speaking, it was not possible. Faithfulness and partnership are high values in the evolution of love, and we want to realize them. They do not require external vows, but they do require inner trust. At some point then, a quiet vow is made in the heart.

In the Bible, the Gospel of John contains the mysterious sentence: "In the beginning was the Word. ... And the Word became flesh and dwelt among us." In Greek "the Word" is called Logos. Logos is the mental-spiritual structure of the world. This structure is forever connected to the "flesh." Logos and Eros are primal forces in the makeup of the world. Everything arose from them. From this perspective we gain a new insight into both the spiritual and the sexual relationship between the genders. The quality of lust thus obviously also entails something spiritual. "And Adam knew Eve his wife" – this sentence from Genesis 4:1 contains the unity of Eros and insight. Love does not make you blind, but seeing, if it is accompanied by a perceiving mind. Anima and Animus, the feminine and the masculine soul, are about to behold each other anew and experience a new joy of cooperation.

If these two images meet on equal terms, a tremendous cosmic force is created – the primal image of love: the birth of a true partnership relationship and culture. It is an eternal image, written into the eternal soul of all people. This mystery exists in reality; it is not a dream, nor is it wishful thinking or an illusion. It exists as a predisposition already in children, and it accompanies us throughout life, provided we remain faithful to it. Even if every hit song in the world has sung about it a thousand times, it is still true that there is nothing more beautiful than love. Kitsch and reality are sometimes so close together.

Eros is the messenger of an endless cosmic and earthly joy. Sexual energy is pure life energy, and wherever sex and love come together, we find what all people long for more than anything else: an embodiment of ecstasy, bliss, a zest for life and the power of action. Sometimes I can only thank Creation for this gift. If we all held this gift in our hands, a wave of infinite gratitude would sweep over our entire planet. One of the goals of a global peace movement is to realize this image of love in the first communities, the first places for a global new future, and the first networks. This would mean the final end of all sexual violence.

Dancing Couple, 2001

4. The Historical Shadow and Its Dissolution

What is so difficult about love, and why is it so seldom fulfilled? Why does almost the whole world seem to be suffering from love-sickness? How has human society managed to turn love, the most beautiful thing in the world, into a source of hatred and violence? Was it a cosmic Satan who wreaked havoc on the world, as described in the old mythologies? Was it the evil Loki, who in the Germanic Götterdämmerung conquered the good God Baldur? What is this Evil in the world? We can only provide the following tentative answer: Evil is a mental power that arose in the human being when they began to leave the sacred order and establish their own systems of power. Evil is the mental-spiritual fallout of a culture of war which was ruthlessly established through the millennia, against all standards of trust and love. As early as when the Egyptian pyramids were being built, the priests fought against the primordial wisdom of the priestesses who came from Malta. In her book Temple of Love, Sabine Lichtenfels describes this ancient knowledge. We can easily recognize it, as soon as we find ourselves in a place where we are free from the clutches of fear. The ancient knowledge is written into the molecular matrix of the nucleus of our cells. We can find it everywhere in the encounter with all people and all our co-creatures.

We are separated from this ancient knowledge by the traumatic knot we find ourselves in as long as we follow the outer and inner control system of the war society. These are the rules of fear, of anger and of constant reaction. The traumatic knot is the sediment of history that is stored in the basement of our subconscious and in the epigenetic structures of our cell nuclei – a subconscious demon who constantly interferes with our current lives. It is a trauma of the entire human race. The task of a new peace movement consists of disempowering the demon, untying the knot and paving the way for the powers of healing and love of the sacred matrix. The Global Healing Biotopes project was born as the result of an unceasing human and political commitment.

Wilhelm Reich wrote a book entitled The Murder of Christ. This refers to a historical event, the crucifixion of Jesus of Nazareth. Let us assume that the story is true. Jesus loved a woman, Mary Magdalene. And this woman loved Jesus wholeheartedly. She then experienced her loved one being nailed to the cross. Do we know what it means to be nailed to a cross alive? What did Mary Magdalene experience in this moment? It was over for her. There was only a helpless pain; from then on everything ceased to exist, her belief in love, her faith in God, her belief in a life in love and truth. Everything disappeared into powerless, ultimate despair. She experienced what millions of others have experienced, from then until today. It is the primal trauma of love destroyed. The social order of the patriarchal era, which is based on power, had to shatter the original connection between love and community in order to produce governable subjects. For century after century, for generation after generation, the tribes and peoples of the Earth were subjected to the same cruel fate.

Let us take a different example from today. A tribal community in the Brazilian jungle is robbed of its livelihood by the lumberjacks of Swedish logging companies. A love couple lives in this Indigenous community. The man goes to the lumberjacks to earn money for himself and the tribe. In the eyes of the tribe, he has thereby betrayed them. A fight ensues and the young man is killed. The young woman had loved him more than anything else and now she is standing there like Mary Magdalene, with a powerless pain with no way out. Whom can she hate? Against whom or what can she transform her pain into rage? Neither against her tribe nor against her loved one. Against the lumberjacks? But most of them are from other, similar tribes. All that remains is her rage against the logging company. But that is part of an imperialist system against which she has no chance. She is left with deep, ultimate resignation – resignation in the face of imperial violence against which an individual or an individual community truly has no chance.

As long as the human being, man and woman, is exposed to the external influence of such powers, love and faith don't stand a chance.

In all countries, whether in Greenland, China,the Philippines,Sudan, the US or Germany – whether in the East, South, West or North – everywhere, the same primal drama of the destruction of love, solidarity and trust is occurring in the name of the only world religion that dominates the world: the religion of global capitalism. But this, too, consists of human beings, who also carry the trauma within themselves. Here, it no longer makes sense to simply accuse and oppose. There is no liberation movement, no leftist politics that can overcome the existing system as long as they insist on the current positions, for they are always – whether from the right or from the left – the positions of an unsolved inner pain, an eternally unfulfilled love and an unresolved inner rage with no way out. They are the positions of a humanity that has deeply learned that love, trust and community always end in catastrophe. It is the hypnosis that permeates our planet, the enormous drop of acetone that constricts the human heart.

Today, the task consists of the liberation from this collective hypnosis: Dehypnotization, re-conditioning, the inner liberation from the belief in the cross. There is only one task for global revolution: liberating love from the cross forever. Only when we begin to understand the collective primal trauma and begin to build a world that is stronger than this power can we achieve liberation and salvation. It is true that ecology and alternative technologies for water, energy and food are a necessary aspect of a new direction of thinking, but they can only become globally effective if we combine these innovations with an inner truth. And that is a truth that lies in the human mental-spiritual area of sex, love, partnership and community.

5. AN IMPENETRABLE WALL

I ask my readers not to lose their belief in goodness and beauty when in the coming passages I have to shine a light on the dark sides of the history we all come from. To realize the paradise we know is possible, we must see and overcome the factors that have so far prevented it.

First, I wish to say that all pain in love constitutes a false reality, delusions and phantom pains from a past that keeps affecting us until we have recognized them and cast them off. All these wounds, these separation anxieties and jealousies, this fury of rage and despair are an eternal inner parroting of things that we believe today because we have experienced them in the past, and because millions of others also have experienced them. We are dealing with an illness which, as is the case for all illnesses, stops immediately when we let go of the delusion. Even paralysed people can rise from their beds if they are released from the hypnosis of their paralysis by a healer (see Mary Rogers, Harry Edwards, Bruno Gröning, Poul Bjerre and many others). Yes, it is truly hypnosis that keeps us believing in what is constantly tormenting us. We need a situation that liberates us from our hypnosis and opens our eyes forever.

In love there is no fear of separation, no competition, no jealousy, no litigation. Once we have pierced through all these levels, when all these inner wars have been ended, and when the projections and fears have been dissolved, we encounter a different reality. We begin to see each other. "And they knew each other." A primal experience of love. "And Adam knew Eve, his wife." Was not the same word in Hebrew used for knowing and making love?

Throughout history, love between the sexes was also a story of unimaginable violence. Women were robbed of their sacred sources of power at the behest of male Gods. Even today they are faced with the choice of adapting to male norms or leading a very lonely life. The problem cannot be solved by the thinking regarding women's liberation we have had so far. We need a new order of life to establish trust between the sexes, an order of life that allows for a free, sincere sexual life for everyone, a life order of trust and solidarity among all those involved.

Love – we have experienced love deeply and unambiguously in blessed magic moments in life. It is a reality that seems to absorb all other realities. But at some point, an impenetrable wall arose, a wall that turned what love had been into its extreme opposite – not only privately for you or me, but everywhere and at all times. The drama, the despair in love, was played out everywhere, in ancient Greece as well as in the metropolises of our times. There was no way out of this irresolvable entanglement. It is the misery of an entire culture, whose inner spaces we hardly dare look into. Millions of young lovers are unable to find a way out of their pain because they live in a social system in which there is no way out. They loved each other, and then they desired someone else. They then had to lie to each other, and the result was distrust, jealousy and separation anxiety. Love turned into its opposite. The vow of fidelity that was supposed to save the relationship instead contributed to its destruction, for in most cases this fidelity could not withstand the sudden rush of the real forces of Eros.

This is the tragedy of our times. Behind the habits of our lifestyles, consumerism and thinking, behind our indifference towards the arms industry and ethnic cleansing, we have the primal tragedy of love. It infects the children. They become suspicious, withdraw or turn into criminals. Society is fully occupied dealing with the many crimes that emerge from despair in love. In the debate about global sexism, it no longer makes sense to complain about endless sexual assaults and acts of violence without understanding the background and recognizing that we live in a society that simply is not up to the task of dealing with the true sexual forces of its own members. The problem not only concerns individual Hollywood celebrities or the young men who use a New Year's celebration to briefly liberate their dammed-up testosterone levels. It concerns the entire population and extends to the highest circles of the church and political leaders in our current society. All of them are affected, whether as perpetrators or victims. Our current society has not dealt with the elementary forces of human sexuality and therefore always carries the unsolved sexual issue in its belly like an explosive minefield. If we wish to build a future world without violence, we must first develop a new social system in which the sexual nature of humans stands a chance of permanently expressing itself, without being corrupted by lies and deception.

The establishment of nonviolent community requires a new image of the relationship between the masculine and the feminine, for the two forces constitute the energetic magnetic field on which all human society is founded.

By suppressing woman, man robbed himself of his source. No man can permanently be happy in a world of unhappy women, and the converse is true for women, too. The human being is in a dead end street in which love can hardly be found anywhere. This epic drama constantly gives rise to global cruelty against humans and animals. A loving person cannot be cruel. Humanity must therefore have the goal of creating an alternative human society that opens the hearts again. The spirit of trust and love gives our organism controlling impulses that no longer allow for any violence.

The rediscovery of love opens up a surprising source of understanding. One can sense something: "Oh, so that was it!" In all sobriety and joy, it could give rise to something like permanent and basic faithfulness, solidarity and cooperation between the genders – a "culture of partnership" as Riane Eisler calls it. I think this was how the plan of Creation was designed.

What works between two people can work for everyone. Getting there may seem difficult but, in spite of all disappointments, it is good to know the direction to head towards. We often go through one relationship after the other before finding the light that briefly shone in each of these relationships. It

is the light of a truly great, even eternal, love. It is a fire in the soul that cannot be extinguished.

6. AVE MARIA – DIE MAN'S FUNDAMENTAL LOVE OF WOMAN AND THE FIGHT AGAINST THIS LOVE

Historically speaking, men are injured when it comes to women. They are magically attracted to the female, but they have not learned to deal with this magic. Instead, they get caught up in contradictions of longing and fear, of natural drives and acquired morals; they get confused and no longer understand themselves. They then often lose it and become pushy, violent, submissive, bossy or moralizing, thereby destroying what they actually love. And yet every man has an archetypal love of the female. Every man loved his mother at some point. Even despots like Adolf Hitler, Saddam Hussein and Vladimir Putin once loved their mothers. Even in the darkest times of the Catholic Church, in the crusades and the Inquisition of the Middle Ages, they worshiped the feminine and sang "Ave Maria." Many gothic cathedrals were named "Notre Dame." And this occurred during a time when woman and lust were regarded as mortal sins and were persecuted to the point of annihilation.

Man still emerges from the body of woman; she is his primal home, his Goddess, his "Holy Grail." He cannot do anything but revere her. But there is a sexual temptation within woman that is not quite compatible with his reverence. He is thus caught in a conflict between spiritual reverence and sexual desire. Historically speaking, he could not handle this conflict. In Goethe's famous love story, The Sorrows of Young Werther, the young Werther was hopelessly in love with his Lotte, but he could not bring this love to life. He could not even tell her what he felt for her, for there are no words to express the power of love and of awakening sexual desire. The result has been innumerable misunderstandings and tragedies, generation after generation.

To be able to rule, man had to curse the flesh and deprive woman of her power. The historical church father Augustine showed the way. He could find no other way to cope with his sexual desires than to permanently demonize them. The humiliation of woman by man, which pervaded the entire patriarchal era, was the result of the male's inability to face woman, whom he so strongly desired, in an appropriate way. The deeper this inner impotence was, the more violently the male power manifested outwardly. Men's brutality was a reaction against the overwhelming power of Eros, which he encountered in the image of the female body.

The patriarchal world was not intent on love, but on war. Men had other things to do than to deal with matters of love; they had to go to war, conquer lands and establish empires. They had to be willing to endure pain, to kill and be killed. This was the only way wars could be won. Every empire, every nation, every boundary has arisen through the insanity of war. A masculine structure developed that was incompatible with the deep, unfulfilled, eternal longing for female love. Woman became a disruptive factor in a male world that was focused on establishing religious, economic and political empires. The subjects had to obey. But what subject willingly obeys if he or she is in love?

The destruction of love was a prerequisite for the creation of modern, imperial societies, for loving people cannot be controlled.

And yet love has endured. Behind all veils we still find the truth of an everlasting love between the genders. There is an archetypal image of the female in every young man, which he – consciously or unconsciously – remains faithful to, no matter how much he may deny it. The woman whom he cannot win for himself becomes the focus of mighty projections. And so, the young man stands shy and awkward in front of the girl he doesn't know how to interact with, because he has elevated and glorified her with his adolescent projection. And yet there is truth in Novalis' words, which he wrote after the early death of his beloved Sophie: "Love is the final purpose of world history – the Amen of the Universe."

Der letzte Harbstbäume
an Helles Teich   DD 17/11/2015

The last fall tree at Helles pond, 2015

7. The Primal Love Between Mother and Son

In the Love School at Tamera we keep encountering the topic of the love of all sons towards their mothers and the mothers towards their sons. The love between mother and son (as well as the daughters' love of their fathers) constitutes one of the elementary powers of life. Here we have a prototype, an archetype of love that needs to be liberated from the repression of a falsely controlled society in order for both sexes to find a healed and purified form of love. (While I am writing this, an enormous hurricane is sweeping across Texas. Is there possibly a connection between the elementary forces of the weather and the elementary forces of Eros?)

In our "deep conversations" that we have in our community in Tamera, we regularly experience how deep the mother-son relationship is. I also knew this from my former practice as a psychoanalyst. There is nothing that the young boy loves more than his mother. A morphogenetic wave of healing and liberation will occur when, in the first communities on Earth, an order of life is created in which the relationship between mother and son can follow the energies of love. For here we find ourselves at the core of the entire causal complex of our crazy world. This relationship largely determines how a man develops in the area of Eros, how he later approaches women and what sexual identity he chooses. This relationship lasts a lifetime, both for the mother and the son, consciously or subconsciously. The mother remains the mother all her life and the son remains the son all his life. This means that if there was true love in this relationship, then this love continues in the adult son and is found in his love for all that is female. But if there were blockages in this relationship, if at some point pain and wounding resulted, usually already in childhood, then these wounds continue to fester in adulthood.

However, as an adult, you always have the possibility to make corrections. We can still give relationships a new, healing direction if we are willing to recognize inner blockages and resolve them through genuine experiences of love.

I loved my mother. For me she was grand and sacred; a kind of Madonna, Magna Mater – the image of the Great Female. As a small son, you could not but love and cherish her, and if she gave you her love openly, then happiness abounded. But my mother, too, was a victim of the taboos of a disoriented society and believed she had to raise us strictly, the way she had been brought up herself. Inwardly, however, she did not like this strictness and, with every beating she gave me, she beat her own heart.

There is no man on Earth who would not love his mother if he – perhaps not until after her death – could see her clearly and recognize her fully. And as for the practically indestructible love of mothers for their sons, there is hardly a woman who would not take her son in her arms, even if he had done the worst of things within the Islamic State or any other terror organization.

Every young (and also older) man experiences the "mother-imago," the sacred Marian image, in a beloved woman, an image that he projects onto the loved one. In Schiller's Song of the Bell we read the following: "Her steps he blushingly doth follow, and is by her fair greeting blessed. The fairest seeks he in the meadow, with which by him his love is dressed." This is not the folly of youth; it is a principle in the divine plan of life. Phases of shyness, confusion or impotence are then not a sign of weakness; they are positive characteristics of the "son-man," who does not yet know how to deal with the awakening power of Eros, and in his reverence and elevation of the female does not know what is allowed and to what extent his longing for a woman is based on reciprocity. Since his mother often appeared as the punishing or negating authority, she not only elicits temptation but also appears as a latent danger that he has to protect himself against. Both women and men suffer from a false sexual culture. This is the beginning of an erotic conflict within the collective of humanity: Man's erotic turmoil and the secret rage of the eternally frustrated woman. One of the women in our "deep conversations" recently said: "I don't want to just be worshiped by these son-men all the time." It's a liberating experience for everyone when such truths can be expressed unadorned in a trusting community.

In this inner conflict between spiritual adoration and sexual desire, the son-man either begins to fight his own impulses or else he begins to fight the female. It is not only an individual fight that is fought in the diaries of a lonesome youth; it is a historical fight that untold thousands of people have fallen victim to. This conflict situation is described dramatically in the story of archangel Michael's "Fight with the Dragon." He must conquer the dragon to gain his freedom. The dragon symbolizes the elementary sexual force of the female primal nature, whose tempting power must be overcome through the fight. But the man can never win this fight, for it is a fight against his own nature.

All advanced civilizations, all patriarchal religions, have followed this sexually oriented image of war against the dragon, and all of them have fought the elementary power with sword and fire. The unimaginable burning of witches during the Middle Ages is only one example from a historical era during which men never developed past the son-man stage and were never allowed to love what they desired most. Man's cruelty towards woman and the body are always a reaction against forbidden love. And yet they prayed to the sacred Mother: Ave Maria! Behind all persecutions and denials, Man's Holy Grail was always the woman – the eternal female. And every male child first experiences this sanctuary within the mother. The healed mother-son relationship holds a key for the final dissolution of the patriarchal madness.

From son-man to man. It is a strange process whereby the soul of a man suddenly realizes that he is truly loved by his mother. What is otherwise said offhandedly becomes an irritating experience of happiness. **If the man steps out of his habitual mother projections and suddenly discovers his mother's love of him and his love** of his mother, then an unusual shift takes place. He forms a new relationship to woman; he becomes her eternally faithful partner.

Without losing any respect or adoration, he no longer projects the almighty mother onto the woman, but recognizes in her his own polar equivalent, his "anima." The two sexes meet as equals. Because they connect in trusting solidarity, he knows what is allowed and what she wants, for she wants the same thing as he does. On his own he finds the forms of inner coherence that are available for the realization of sensual and spiritual love. Both sexes are now within the system of the sacred matrix. Both recognize the ethical principles of Eros, love and partnership that govern this system. Both of them will find that their old thoughts of separation, fear of abandonment and jealousy are dissolved all by themselves.

Within such a life order of people who trust each other, no mother will allow her son to go to war. The redemption of the son-men is at the same time the redemption of the mothers.

8. A Daughter's Primal Love of Her Father

Spectacular scenes are played out when women in a group speak openly about their love towards their fathers. Almost every woman in our circles had a strong bond with her father as a child; all they wanted was to sit in his lap, listen to his stories or soak up his adoration. Also as an adult, the love of a man can make a woman's heart soar. Whether consciously or unconsciously, an adult woman seeks qualities in a man that are similar to the ones she loved in her father. The man, who is not aware of these things, is then surprised at her exaggerated devotion or her aggressive reactions. In most cases he cannot fulfill this "father imago," for he is a son-man himself, looking for the mother in her. This is a disastrous situation. Two adult lovers, a woman and a man, come together. She is like a daughter, seeking a strong man, whereas he is like a son seeking in her the mother. That's not a good fit. There's constant chafing and grating between them and they don't know why. Who is to blame for this? Patriarchy, the social dominance of men, the doctrine of an almighty Father God? Or is there more to it than meets the eye?

There was a time in our community when we no longer wanted any male Gods. Religion was supposed to liberate itself from the patriarchal grip. Instead of saying "God," we said "Goddess." Then a courageous woman appeared and protested against this transformation. She wanted the male God, the Father, the Savior. Why? As a small girl – like most girls – she had a deep connection with her father. He was the head of the family; he seemed to know everything and could do anything; he was always busy doing important things and was only rarely at home. This opened the door wide for female projection. The father was the embodiment of male power and wisdom, the goal of eternal longing. In the course of patriarchal history, this gave rise to an all-powerful father-imago, which today is active within all women when searching for their prince, the strong man, in whose arms they feel secure.

Today, we recognize these connections without contempt or irony, for they are real connections between the sexes in the archetypal world of the human soul. The positive image of the father is not only the result of a patriarchal aberration; instead, it is rooted in the architecture of the soul of all humans, not only women. But in the female soul it is connected with a deep longing for devotion. Mechthild von Magdeburg thus said: "Ah Lord, love me deeply and love me often and love me long!" It is truly a primal desire of the female soul. There will come a time when emancipated men will be able to recognize, love and fulfill this female desire, without contempt, abuse or degradation. And there will come a time in which emancipated women will gladly put themselves into the hands of the new men. For both sexes belong together forever. A part of the home of woman lies with man – and a large part of the home of man lies with woman. These are the structures of life in the healing space of the sacred matrix.

Modern women have done a lot to liberate their female soul from desiring a man. But they, too, once loved and admired this male authority that they fight today. If they had had fathers who loved and protected them beyond all patriarchal structures, the debate about emancipation would today be very different. A political feminism would probably also have emerged, but a different one that is no longer directed against men, but against a system in which no loving maleness and no loving femaleness is possible. Many women's anger against men is the result of a world in which there were no men they could trust unconditionally. A man who a woman could trust permanently hardly existed on Earth. Conversely, men had a similar problem with women (see previous chapter). They were son-men and therefore hardly able to present this positive image of a man. Behind the fight between the sexes, the same tragedy is constantly being lived out, whereby we seek something in the other that cannot be found there. This drama will only be solved by becoming aware of these connections and by creating new social systems in which these topics can be recognized under the protection of a community. Intelligent people are beginning to no longer react to this entire situation with private anger or resignation, but with insight, trust and deep solidarity.

Today, there are a growing number of groups and communities on Earth in which the topic is seen and experienced in a much deeper way than in the world of media and public discussion. Today, both women and men are engaged in a process of inner development that allows them to recognize and resolve the traumatic connections mentioned above. Only when both genders are able to meet each other on an equal footing, without putting each other on pedestals and without the familiar rage and anger, can this warped world return to its natural order.

9. Eros and Religion

A wave of healing will pass through all of evolution as soon as the first human beings and communities are able to harmonically combine the sexual and spiritual core forces of life. In our cultural tradition to date, the forces of religion and spirituality were outside the bodily forces of sex and Eros. The split between mind and body was incredibly deep within almost all religious movements, even in the texts of such widely read books as A Course in Miracles. Renouncing the body and solely turning to spirit is the historical reaction to the difficulties with sensual love. In Confessions, St. Augustine, the church father mentioned above, described this process in detail. He was so besieged by the demon of sex that he could only conquer it through a total ban. Herein lies the true origin of the contempt of sexuality: It was simply too powerful. Against this psychological background, the prescribed cruel punishment of female sexuality, the stonings and witch burnings, appear in a different light.

A new relationship between Eros and religion is definitely and forever a part of the new matrix. By "religion," I do not mean what has been passed down to us; I mean a form of reunified life. Religion and Eros both come from the same primal source of life. There, heavenly love and erotic life are forever united. As German cultural philosopher Walter Schubart writes in Religion and Eros: "The forces of religion and sexuality are the two strongest forces of life. Those who see them as primal opponents teach the eternal ambivalence of the soul. Those who see them as irreconcilable enemies tear apart the human heart. And it has been torn apart! Anyone reflecting on religion and Eros must put their finger on one of the most painful wounds that are bleeding in the depth of the human heart."[1]

If we look at the sexual and religious history of humanity, we recognize the continuous discrepancy between these two forces of life. As

---

[1] English translation by the translator

"Ecce Homo", watercolor, 1987

long as this opposition exists, there can be no planetary peace. Religion and Eros must come together. Religion without Eros becomes cold, dogmatic and fanatic. Eros without religion becomes obsessive or boring. When Eros and religion come together, the boundaries between the two are dissolved and both of them gain new content. We experience the same primal happiness at the primal religious source as at the erotic one. On a healed planet there will no longer be a religion that defends itself against Eros, nor any religions that distance themselves from other religions. They will not even be called "religions," for it is the sacred itself that emerges from all life, and the sacred is the same everywhere on Earth. Defend the Sacred!

I do not belong to any existing religion. I come from a Christian family, but already as a young man I left the church. And yet in the Christian church as well as in other religions I see renewal movements with which we can cooperate in the name of a humane world. The large world religions have fought sexual love, but – as is the case for all religions – they originally emerged from a fundamental human experience. It is the experience of a primal, sacred power in Creation that we have called "God." This sacred power exists immanently in life and in all beings. We are all connected with it, with the sacred matrix of the One Life; otherwise we could not live. May the thoughts expressed in this book contribute to connecting love with this source. This is also true for the ideas about free sexuality that are described in this book.

Reuniting Eros with the sacred is a key to the rebirth of a humane society.

We can experience this reunion of Eros with the sacred, the "original wedding night" known as "Hieros Gamos" (Holy Marriage), with a single partner, but what it refers to goes even further to include the overall co-existence of the two sexes. Here, in the depth of the soul and the body, is where the spiritual transformation occurs, the "metanoia," the "Gnostic leap," first for individual communities and then for the whole world. And here, deep in the body, we find woman's longing, and the longing of all flesh, for salvation and fulfillment. This is the very real point where the decision is made if the apocalypse leads to destruction or healing. There is a point in the relationship between the sexes where the decision for war or peace on Earth is made. This point has to do with the final recognition of our inveterate sexual nature and of the female source that only radiates warmth and love if it is no longer threatened or denied.

The healing of love is not limited to sexual love. It also encompasses a new relationship to all our fellow creatures. We need to reintegrate our human world into the overall world of life, in order to heal our primal pain of separation. Ultimately, this constitutes reconnecting with "Omega," the divine center of all things. The Jesuit father and paleontologist Teilhard de Chardin once said that "To love is to approach each other center to center." The more we open our eyes, the more we see in our love partners the outlines of a sacred being. We can call it the "being of Christ." I have realized that this being shines through wherever trust occurs. Every human soul seems to have this being as its own "entelechial" or sacred image at its core. In this sense, to be seen means to be loved. The communities of the future could consist of people who have seen this gestalt in each other. There can be no enmity between them. It was this inner gestalt, or image, that we all discovered in each other in the blissful time when we first fell in love. For the young man, the idolized girl is heaven itself:

"Blushing he follows her tracks. And is made blissful by her greeting ...." (Friedrich von Schiller).

During such experiences we projected something onto each other that actually was inside of us. We glorified each other, and this glorification contained the inkling of a coming lust, both physical and spiritual. Even after all the disappointments, we retain the possibility of working towards this image of love until we no longer need any projections because it has been realized in real love.

10. What is the Sacred Matrix?

There is a world order in the Universe that is based on unity, trust and love – we call it the "sacred matrix." It is not a simple pipe dream by us humans, but an objective structure in the blueprint of Creation. The sacred matrix is the original, transhistorical, cosmic or divine order of universal life. It appeared to us in childhood when the candles burned on the Christmas tree; it filled us with the bliss of first love; and it is operating in the germination of a seed, in the division of cells and in the birth of a crystal. Sometimes it looks out, pure and clear, from the eyes of an infant. And sometimes – in the deepest moments of compassion – it reaches our heart. Then, for a brief eternity, we are transformed, and we know the goal of our journey.

There is a movie we can all watch on the internet – "The Man who Swims with Crocodiles." It is about the love between a man and a crocodile. The two are connected in an intimacy that is so tender that one can hardly imagine it between people. The man's kiss on the mouth of the adult crocodile seems so otherworldly that one cannot believe it until one sees it. However, this story is not otherworldly; it is earthly and real. But it is outside of all acquired concepts and projections of fear. This is not a unique story. It is confirmed by innumerable further animal research examples. The blueprint of Creation contains the holy alliance of life, and this includes a deep love between humans and animals. In Tamera we have experienced many small similar examples. At night, Simon (9 years of age) encounters a wild boar with her young ones and remains free of fear – he tries to pet it. (This scene happened to have been filmed.) When the next day one of his fellow classmates asked him why he wasn't afraid, he said: "The wild boar is just like us." Whereupon his young friend says: "Then I want to care for the wild boar with you in Tamera." Another example: Aron, 6 years old, stumbles over a terrier who is bound to a post and who snaps at him violently. After crying out briefly, the boy says: "The dog is not evil; he was just as startled as I was." Here, a kind of contact with animals is described that opens a new door to the integration of our human life into the large family of all creatures.

All these real events show the (latent) existence of a different world in which there is no fear and no enmity. They show what life is capable of if it is not destroyed by the interference of fear and violence. It is the world of the sacred matrix, which lies behind everything as a real possibility and is waiting to be called upon. We have not invented this world; it was here long ago in Indigenous peoples that were not subject to the patriarchal system and could therefore retain the original symbiosis between human beings and nature. It still exists today, in Indian villages where 3,000 inhabitants live together with almost as many cobras; and in tribes in Borneo, where men, women and children walk barefoot through the jungle and pray for the protection of nature, of the trees, of snakes and of all living souls. An especially beautiful example is the Indian Bishnoi community, where people live together with wild animals in such trust that we must permanently put aside our prejudices. There is no limit to the friendship between humans and animals, provided it is not destroyed by humans.

This world is the entelechial basic pattern of life, the goal of a new planetary civilization. This world is potentially a love affair. Love is the highest cultural heritage and the sacred aspect of existence. Its genetic basis is written into the nuclei of our cells; it is the core information of all life. Everything strives for unity. Teilhard de Chardin wrote: "Driven by the forces of love, the fragments of the world seek each other so that the world may come into being."

Can we imagine new communities arising on Earth in which we humans grow up in such friendship with our fellow creatures? Can we imagine a world in which the concept of enmity has disappeared completely? Are we able to identify and create the ethical, social, ecological and spiritual preconditions for such a world to actually emerge? Is it not an obvious thought to begin with such an attempt?

If we today develop digital weapon systems that can destroy any enemy, could we not also develop systems of life in which no weapons are needed, because our passions are guided by a higher power? We are currently experiencing the emergence of an international network that is intent on realizing this idea. We have given it the name "Terra Nova." This idea is not tied to a special group, but to the world information of the sacred matrix. This information is everywhere, even in the smallest gestures of connectedness.

What is the sacred? A world in which people stick together and care for each other, even when they are in distress – that is a part of the sacred. A world in which children can fully trust their parents and all adults – that is a part of the sacred. A world in which the sexual attraction between two people no longer produces fear, jealousy and hatred in a third person – that is a part of the sacred. A world in which the animals come up to people because we bid them welcome and they no longer have to be afraid of us – that is a part of the sacred. A world in which we perceive and care for the Earth and the water as living organisms – that is a part of the sacred. When refugee workers stretch out their hand to save a drowning person – that is a part of the sacred. When active peace workers find the necessary peace in the middle of their work with crisis and conflict to gather in a sacred space, then that is a part of the sacred. And when people pray for a terminally ill person who then recovers – then the sacred has performed one of its innumerable miracles.

We do not necessarily need to call it "God," for the sacred has no name. It is the inner power that brings us all together and forever connects us with all our fellow creatures. What is shown in the love story between a human being and a crocodile is really a planetary topic. It is incredibly far-reaching. The sacred matrix contains a possibility of salvation that we first have to get used to. It is as "otherworldly" and at the same time as real as the love between a human being and a crocodile. And yet we deeply sense the truth and the possibility of such a planetary love affair. We sense that such a world of love could exist and that we can realize it if we agree on it. If it succeeds in one place, then it can succeed everywhere.

The sacred alliance of life encompasses all beings; all are connected to this basic pattern, and all carry this image like a primal memory in their souls. It is built into humanity's entelechial program. When a group of people create a new life order according to the sacred matrix, they activate an image of life which is (latently) present in all human beings. As soon as the image is realized in real-life practice, it can be received everywhere, for then the collective consciousness of humanity enters an "excited state." There are sensors everywhere that receive the image and there are forces waiting to implement it, for the image is understood and loved at a cellular level. This is part of the secret of healing through contact with the healing stream of life. A sick child can get well when a little dog lies down beside it.

This concept provides the design for a paradise of a new Earth; it is the concrete utopia of a humanity that has permanently left the old field of enmity and violence behind. Time and again, we need to question the facts and test reality around us to recognize that this utopia is not a dream or an illusion, but a message concerning a different form of culture on our planet that is written into the genetic material of all beings.

Today we are at a turning point in history. A knowledgeable part of humanity knows that there can be no permanent community, no planetary liberation, unless we reconnect with the higher level of order from which we all came. At first this is a slow, growing process within individual groups and within newly created global networks, but the process accelerates as more people on Earth realize and implement it. From a certain point on, it will go very fast. Because – and this is worth repeating a thousand times – all human beings are connected to this enormous power of transformation through their higher nature. Then Jerusalem could perhaps truly be transformed into a sacred city. The miracle of liberation will no longer be a pipe dream, but a morphogenetic wave that rolls across the Earth.

11. The Story of the Fall

The world of patriarchal religions created a strong taboo against woman and against the body. Already the story of the so-called "Fall" shows this repression in a frighteningly direct way. The serpent seduces Eve into picking the apple. She gives it to Adam, who then "knows" her, which means that they make love physically. The almighty God then chases them out of paradise and subjects them to terrible punishments. It is hard to believe what it says in the catastrophic passages in the Old Testament, for example in Genesis 3:14–19. I quote from the New International Version of the Bible:

"So the Lord God said to the serpent, 'Because you have done this, cursed are you above all livestock and all wild animals! You will crawl on your belly and you will eat dust all the days of your life.'" (Verse 14)

"'And I will put enmity between you and the woman, and between your offspring and hers; he will crush your head, and you will strike his heel.'" (Verse 15)

"To the woman he said, 'I will make your pains in childbearing very severe; with painful labor you will give birth to children. Your desire will be for your husband, and he will rule over you.'" (Verse 16)

The serpent, the sign on the Aesculapian staff, initially a symbol of sexuality and healing, is to be crushed. Eve, who in the beginning was deeply connected to the loving serpent power of all life, is now to separate herself from her primal nature and stomp on the serpent's head. And the man shall be her lord. That's what it actually says; it is a "divine" order – in the beginning of a worldwide Judeo-Christian cultural development! Billions of people have believed in it. How can a humane culture ever arise under such conditions?

What does this story mean? Why did the omnipotence of sexual love have to be replaced by the brutal omnipotence of a punishing God? Why did religion have to be used against love? The empire of religion that men created at that time required its subjects to obey, and the anarchic power of Eros did not fit into the system of patriarchal power. Again: People who encounter each other in true love cannot be controlled. Nor will they go to war. No mother would let her sons go to war if she lived in a loving world. A prerequisite for wielding male, imperial power was always the suppression of love. There is a continuous line from the biblical Fall and the Inquisition during the Middle Ages to the cruel actions of today's intelligence services and terrorist movements. Violence is the result of the suppression of life forces. The history of the existing systems is a history of suppressed sexuality. In order to save himself from his cruel God and comply with his laws, man created an arsenal of teachings, religions and moral laws, which from then on were to constitute the core of human culture. A patriarchal society arose, with its Pharisees, priests and cardinals. The long cultural fight against woman and the body – stonings, mutilations, the burning of witches at the stake – made it impossible for practically every woman to reveal herself regarding sexual matters. The old story of the Fall left brutal scars on humanity that are visible to this day.

The biblical story of the Fall is itself a result of a religious aberration; it is itself the Fall. The so-called "sin" consisted of Adam and Eve doing something that all people most like to do. They "knew" each other in the pleasure and desire of their bodies. Since they were so terribly punished for it, they had to do it secretly; they had to lie. They could not find a way out, and since they were continuously threatened by the presence of a terrible God and his henchmen priests on Earth, they themselves began to persecute and hate what they had once loved. This is a nameless tragedy that courses through thousands of years of history. Strong, committed and intelligent work is needed to heal this wound at the center of our culture. If we succeed in this work, human evolution will embark on a new direction and human society will have a new ethical orientation. A new chapter in the story of Creation would begin: Genesis Two – Terra Nova.

12. Sexuality and Violence

Love is the "Archimedean point" of life – the point at which Archimedes said that one could lift the Earth off its foundation if one were given the location of this point and a long enough lever.

How can one say this in a world so full of hatred and violence?

It must be said precisely for that reason. Hatred and violence can only exist as long as the sources of a fearless life – trust and love – have run dry. Nothing is crueler than love betrayed. The biographies of sex murderers or historic despots reveal the very deep connection between betrayed love (often already in the parental home) and violence. On the other hand, we find the equally certain connection between true love and kindness, humanity and standing up for life. Could a young man who has just made love to a girl, kill a rabbit?

No ISIS fighter would kill a person if he had grown up in a loving world.

We need to know this. Please read Alice Miller's life stories of the despots of the 20th century. They would probably not have become despots if their lives had not early on been darkened by rejection and hatred.

Jürgen Bartsch was one of the most famous sex murderers in German criminal history. He was barely 16 when he abducted four youths, one after the other, to a cave, where he murdered them brutally. At the time (1968) I was asked to write a forensic report about it. I then wrote a longer text entitled "Jürgen Bartsch Within us." It was not just the psychogram of an individual sex murderer, but the psychogram of an entire society that brought forth such sadistic excesses. It is a structure that is inherent in the majority of the male part (partly also the female part) of the population and usually remains limited to inconspicuous emotions and fantasies: the structure of sadomasochism. This issue kept turning up in the in-depth sessions in my previous psychoanalytic practice and in the groups and communities that followed. It was not foreign to me, for I recognized it from my own masturbation fantasies during puberty. Later too, as an adult, I sometimes secretly used such fantasies to reach a sexual climax with a woman. During the course of my further sexual development and experience, they disappeared by themselves. For all those who cannot get rid of their fantasies, it may be important to know that they usually disappear all by themselves if one has the opportunity to let the dammed-up energies flow forth in a trusting contact with partners. The best remedy for this is love. Wherever sexual and spiritual love is present, violence no longer makes sense and no longer resonates.

Inspired by my own fantasies and the healing work with others, I understood what is inherent in human beings and what they are capable of when they – for example, in war – find themselves in a situation where all dams break. Human history to date has been a history of war, and war history has always been a story of limitless sexual violence. When the Russians entered Berlin at the end of the Second World War, an estimated 90,000 women were raped. But this was in no way a Russian peculiarity. Just look at what the obedient soldiers in the German army did in the Greek villages.

The Second World War has officially ended, but sexual violence has not. It is unbelievable what happens in bourgeois circles and keeps escalating. Child porn circulates in worldwide networks, connected to the best and most well-known addresses in civil society, and much, much more. If, within the framework of a thorough crackdown, all sexual delinquents were to be put in jail, then half of humanity would be behind bars.

To summarize: Sexual violence is a global issue of our time. It ranges from international child abuse, the trafficking of women and girls and sadomasochistic private bunkers, to the methods used by the secret services or the Islamic State. In reality, it happens in every civilized society, including in thousands of marriages and families.

A core issue of enlightened peace and healing work is the dissolution of violence and the humanization of our animal desires. Humanization does not mean repression, but revelation and affirmation within a trusting contact. It means encountering trust when one wants to abandon oneself to lust. At this point, almost every woman encounters a subconscious disaster horizon, the fear of an abyss, ingrained by the cruel sword that religions have aimed at the lust of the flesh.

Sex is the most intimate, most denied and most untamable area of our virtual inner world. It is an area that can erupt at any time and then lead to the cruelest perversions that today are common in all social classes. And yet, sexual love could be the greatest bliss in life, as well as a deep source of revelation and healing. We humans must tap into these sources, open them up and liberate them from all cruelty. This is a prerequisite for the development of a loving culture.

Having been misled for millennia through violence and repression, we have engaged in a fundamental denial of reality in two aspects of human existence: sexuality and religion. This has given rise to a cultural canon that still holds us in an iron grip today. It is based on the taboo of sexuality and the taboo against divine revelation. To this day, one can hardly speak of these two areas. But we are called to recognize and overcome both taboos so as to initiate the creation of a global field. Here, "overcoming" does not entail explosive emotions or dogmatic violence, but a growing understanding stemming from real trust between people. Real trust is thus an indispensable prerequisite for our further evolution.

Today, the animal level of the sexual body is hidden beneath deep layers of shame. This has to do with an uninhibited abandonment to the flesh; it is the passionate "Take me" and the amoral self-forgetfulness of two bodies united in true lust. It is the deepest layer of the bodily and female Eros. Here lie the roots of all variations of sadomasochism. Since the sexes have never really been allowed to reveal this level of their desires in the course of history, the most elementary stage of sexuality has suffered the most terrible, violent distortions. Subjected to a biblical curse (in the story of the Fall), the sexual, carnal lust was to the greatest degree destroyed, damned, punished, suppressed and ignored. See the work of Barry Long and Clarissa Estés. When the trauma in this layer is dissolved, a new era will begin for woman, as well as for man. The sexual body is a primal source of female life, and for the man it is the greatest gift that nature could give him.

13. Sexuality is a World Power

Sexuality has always been the number one topic, and still is today. Sexual longing is equally present for both sexes. Every human being with a soul wants the same thing. Peggy Parnass acknowledged this, and Erica Jong traveled the world searching for the one great experience she called the "zipless fuck" (in her book Fear of Flying). We are grateful for her beauty and her honesty. Sexuality controls the human world, both in mythology and reality.

Sexuality led to the so-called Fall of Adam and Eve. Sexuality between Abraham's wife Sarai and the Egyptian Pharaoh determined the political direction of history. Sexuality – through the abduction of Helen – lay behind the fight over Troy. When Europa, the daughter of the Phoenician king, was abducted by Zeus in the form of a bull, sexuality opened the way from the Phoenician to the European culture. Sexuality was the power that caused Elisabeth Haich to fail in her Egyptian initiation (see her book Initiation). Sexuality was the power of the old hierodules, the temple prostitutes in ancient Greece, and the secret of the Attic Goddess with the pomegranate. Sexuality increased the connection between Jesus and Mary Magdalene, his closest initiate. Sexuality lies behind the Koran in which the believers, who fall in a sacred war, are promised all the joys of sensuality in the hereafter. Sexuality was the tragic destiny of Abelard and Heloise. Sexuality is a motive of modern tourism, from Majorca to Thailand. What is this sexuality they are all seeking? What world secret has the power to guide the entire history of the world? What happened in the forests, the huts and the beds? What did man and woman discover together? Why do modern people panic when they discover that their love partners made love with another person? Because they suspect that they enjoyed a kind of lust that their partner cannot find with them. The panic and the horror come from carnal lust.

One does not have to be Sigmund Freud and open one deep psychological window after the other; all we need to do is connect with ourselves and open all our senses. Then we automatically discover the hidden omnipresence of the numinous power we call sexuality. It is the power of an eternally hidden, disclaimed, and secret longing. Even behind the most glaring sexual depictions of our times we find the misery of unfulfilled longing. What appears to be so free is like a whitewashed lust over an ocean of unhappiness. One can easily understand why human history to date could not attain its humane goal: It did not listen to the cry of our bodies and souls.

In his book The Secret Diary of Don Juan, the novelist Douglas Carlton Abrams lets Don Juan reveal the following secret: "I will tell you the reason for my success, and it is not the reasons that have been given – not wealth, nor title, nor beauty. The only secret I have used to unlock the bedchambers of the women I have known is their unquenched thirst for life. The greatest power in the world, greater than kings and popes, is the desire of women. Love, the priests tell us, rules the heavens, but does desire not rule the Earth? One who understands the workings of desire understands the very secret of life."

Eros is not the individual quality of a person or a private relationship. It is an omnipresent world power. Therefore, if it is diverted from its course, it cannot simply be healed through individual therapy. Instead, we need to develop a mental-spiritual resilience that ensures we do not too quickly succumb to our spontaneous wants or needs. All too often, the hasty question "What's in it for me?" blocks the inner process that we need today to get to the bottom of the issue. Before we can harvest something truly useful that is sustainable, we need to recognize the contextual connections that we are all involved in.

So far, when discussing ecological issues, we have thought of global issues such as water, weather and energy. It is high time that we find sustainable solutions to the inner topics of our lives, for all external sustainability will crumble if it lacks an inner human foundation.

This insight alone opens up a new horizon of interpretation for our own questions and conflicts: Our problems are not only our own private problems; they can be found everywhere in many different forms and can only be understood collectively. We can now to a certain extent liberate ourselves from the idea of personal failure: we no longer need to solve everything immediately. Neither do we need to run around feeling depressed because we are not able to deal with the topics of free sexuality and partnership. We can still take part in the great consciousness work for healing.

Even if we are occasionally still jealous, we can remember that jealousy is not a part of love, and even if we are not fully healed, we can know that love is the deepest healing message.

An essential point in inner development is precisely the fact that we no longer need to be the measure of all things and can let go of our own navel-gazing and see the dawn rise above everything. We cannot fight individually against the overpowering misguided erotic powers that today control the entire globe; it would only lead to our own ruin. But we can know that there are healing powers in the universe that, by themselves, guide the topic of Eros in a new direction if we cooperate with them. These are powers both in the visible and invisible world.

In a state of trust, the ethical, mental and spiritual world order of the sacred matrix opens up. All beings are genetically connected with this order, even if they have abandoned it in the course of history. The Archimedean point for the realization of this order is a deeply recognized love. We are all on our way towards it, and we should know that it exists. It is the goal of almost all human longings. Unfulfilled longings are no sentimentality, but a sign pointing towards our inherent, entelechial direction. There is no short-term recipe or formula to achieve the desired fulfillment. Free sexuality, as it has long been practiced in our project, is also not a final solution, but only an indispensable prerequisite for truth. Love is as indefinable as every mystery in life – as indefinable as God. At the same time, it is a world power that moves all of humanity.

14. THE PROBLEM OF RELATIONSHIP

Do we really believe that we can capture the world power of Eros in a private love relationship? This constitutes a historical error that has created more misery than anything else, generating confusion that has led us into an insolvable dilemma. Naomi Klein once wrote: "There is a solution, but not within the system." Could this also apply to love? The statement would then be: "There is a solution for the relationship conflict, but not within the relationship."

What we call "relationship" is a disastrous thing. Two people fall in love and then they retire into their own private happiness and live in a cozy togetherness that undergoes surprising transformations. It begins with romance and blissful devotion. Then everyday life enters into the picture and the romance is not quite as romantic; the sexual paradise is not quite as deep, leading to something like secret disappointment. The two continue to promise to be faithful and secretly hope that the other one keeps their promise. In the long run this cannot go well, for both of them experience the desire to be "unfaithful" – either as something to fear or hope for – and they must hide it from each other. From now on we have a mixture of love and mistrust, and they begin to mutually observe each other. This brings about precisely what they have feared: the other's breach of fidelity, the sexual affair that they fear because they are not free of such thoughts themselves, confirming what they fear most. This is a classic example of a regularly occurring self-fulfilling prophecy.

In a relationship, two people look at each other and relate their actions to each other. They always react to what the other one is doing or not doing, thereby entangling themselves in a mutual cocoon that at some point will explode in anger or despair. They don't know why, so they cannot tell each other why, for they have sworn fidelity to each other. Whenever two people are fixated on each other, as is the case everywhere, there are problems and conflicts. Since both of them are fixated on themselves, they believe they can solve their conflicts among themselves. But deeper love conflicts cannot be solved privately, between two people, for their conflicts are the conflicts of all of humanity. Mutual recriminations then make no sense; instead, they lead to an eternal ping-pong game between two disappointed souls.

The human trauma of love is activated whenever lovers wish to enter into a permanent relationship, yet haven't learned to follow the real laws of love.

As long as they relate their problems to each other, they are shackling themselves emotionally with no escaping.

This often leads to a disastrous development: Silence, quiet hatred and open violence. The world is full of it. No hatred is worse than that between lovers who have sworn fidelity to each other and then feel betrayed and deceived by their partner.

Every couple relationship – even in the best of communities – can at times experience emotional clashes. Eventually, the secret, bottled-up rage explodes for one of them. If this happens without the protection of a group, it can be catastrophic. Many terrible things have happened this way. Here, we need a helping group. One of the ethical rules of a community of trust is that they see such catastrophes coming and prevent them early on. It does not matter what has happened; if someone has reached an emotional boiling point, they should not be lectured and reminded of ethical principles, for that only makes everything worse. Instead, they should first be allowed to show their anger, whether "justified" or not. Although a principle of a spiritual life is to never act out of affect, there are situations in which even the most civilized person flies off the handle. If this happens within a circle of friends and without violence, it can be a healing process. After that they can calmly see and correct their mistake – and perhaps apologize to their partner. They then have the opportunity to solve their conflict in an emotionally cleansed atmosphere within the circle of a supportive group. This "therapeutic" behavior of a group is an important principle when creating humane life systems.

The systemic error in relationships lies in the fixation on one another; the solution lies in undoing this fixation. The eyes of the two partners are then no longer focused on each other, but look parallel into the world, focusing on a joint goal or on the community they are part of, or on social and ethical issues that apply to everyone. If they are part of a social or political movement, they begin to get interested in the fate of other beings, other individuals and peoples. They begin to realize that there is a world outside of their relationship, a world they can participate in and ultimately must participate in. They increasingly discover the backgrounds and goals of their own existence and they become aware of the endless misery on Earth. But they also discover the wonders of nature, they sense the presence of something divine, the secrets of the universe and the logic of healing. They discover this together and thereby find a shared level that lies outside their I-and-you relationship. They thereby gain a power they did not have before – the power of permanent solidarity and partnership – for from now on they together look out into the same world, a higher task and a higher goal. They are now inspired by a joint cause outside of their own private sphere. They feel and know more and more clearly that love is not a private pleasure but a gift to help others.

The loving couples who come to Tamera gain an inner cohesion if they are able to let go of their fixation on each other and in some way participate in the great work of global assistance and healing. They have the opportunity of getting to know each other anew within the framework of this larger issue, without immediately reacting to each other. They now enter into a new phase of their relationship: They discover each other without speaking much about it and begin to trust and truly love each other. This is then without fixation or projection, and they both perceive each other in real solidarity and support. From now on they enter a second level of love. Their friendship increases their ability to deal with conflict, and the conflicts that still sometimes emerge can no longer break their loyalty to each other. This used to be what in the past was meant by a "marriage."

From now on the two of them no longer need to suffer from separation anxiety or jealousy.

15. A SECOND LEVEL OF LOVE

Something very strange has happened there. They "saw" each other. In the middle of the hustle and bustle they began to "see" each other: their movements, their beauty, their truth, their seriousness. It was a long and deep process of recognition that went to the core of their beings. In this beauty an inner portal opened up to something eternal. The vow of eternal love enters the cells; it is this one and only affirmation to remain faithful to the beauty of the loved one and not to let anything distract from this faithfulness. This event is not tied to any gender; it can just as well occur between two men or two women. It is always this power that shines like a divine light in their relationship. If it occurs between a woman and a man, the very special primal quality of polarity is added. You may now deeply and fully love the soul who looks out at you from your polar half. For she is you, but in a different guise, just as she has found you within herself ever more clearly. What an incredible common bond; what a renewal of life!

Finding this love with another person is part of the miracle of life. And yet it is there for everyone. We all participate in this stream of life. What you experience with one person or another opens your heart for many others. Love makes you "seeing," and it is "like a ball of fire that has to be passed on" (Claire Niggli). What happens here between two people opens a door to all people. What is looking at you through those eyes? What deity is so close that it can show itself so tenderly and almost unveiled? What secret is so close to being revealed so easily? It came like a miracle and one could almost hear a voice behind it, saying: "Take the black stone and bless it for your love. What good you have done to each other, you have done to Me, too. You are my opening into the world. Pass on what you have received. May it sparkle in dew drops and leaves, in children's eyes and glasses of wine. May it radiate back from your words, actions and songs. May the shorelines of your lakes, the paths that you walk, the places you visit, the pine trees under which you make love speak of it."

I chose this poetic form to hint at the music of the soul that can arise when love enters into life. When this occurs between a man and a woman, then the heart is in flames. One is in the middle of the mystery of Creation that everyone is seeking. One understands what was originally meant by the terms "wedding" and "marriage." One immediately recognizes that the longing of all human beings is directed towards this beauty and that the origin and goal of love is the same as the Alpha and Omega of life itself — and that all life on Earth is meant to exude this beauty and this love. As Sigmund Freud said, love is the relationship to beauty, and beauty is the authentic, sincere and undistorted gestalt of a person. What a great promise! One is never more grateful than at the moment of this insight. If two lovers are ready to have this experience, and if they do not get stuck in the old trap of false fixation, they will become a blessing for the world.

16. The Intimacy of Truth

In the Tamera community we use a tool called SD Forum. "SD" is the German abbreviation for "Selbstdarstellung," which means something like "self-expression" or "self-presentation." A participant goes into the middle of the group and shows what he or she is feeling and thinking. There is no judgment. Sometimes someone says or does something surprising, such as when a big, husky fellow that everyone admired suddenly says: "I was always afraid of women, and I still am. I pretend to be virile, but I'm not. I'm asking you for help." These are moments of truth. Suddenly the energy in the room changes. The entire group is immediately attentive, it breathes differently, the inner dialogs stop and the joint attention is directed at an issue that concerns everyone. It is the intimacy of truth that now connects us with each other. The more such experiences occur in a community, the more reliably it embraces the ethics of a deep human solidarity.

The fact that our Tamera project still exists and is going strong after four decades is also because in the beginning we created such spaces for truth. We had to learn a lot to be able to do this. When 35 years ago, in our first community in Leuterstal in Southern Germany, we instituted a "week of truth," the 14 participants went at each other with truths to the extent that the days were filled with anger and fear. The result was that six members left the group. The concept of truth had been deeply misunderstood. The participants used their days to vent their pent-up frustrations and aggressions and to say what they thought of each other. But to say what one thinks of each other is not yet an inner truth. Truth arises when we ourselves become true and take off the masks which we use to present images of ourselves to others. Truth means to authentically step out from old role patterns and be willing to let the others look into one's soul. This gives rise to a human involvement and compassion that silences all reflexes of judgment and rejection. Truth creates acceptance and love. To be seen is to be loved. This is also true in the institution of our deep conversations in the group. As soon as the channel between the facilitator and the respondent opens, the person becomes visible in his or her pure gestalt — one could almost say in their Christ image. This opens the door to love, which gives rise to full acceptance. It is an intimacy, not only on the emotional but also the spiritual level, a deep intimacy of being made of the same "stuff."

We find this intimacy in truth to also be present in sexuality, in the erotic and spiritual-emotional structure of a love relationship, just as soon as the two partners have succeeded in leaving their customary network of inner comments and projections aside and mutually recognize their original beauty. Truth is the light of love. The beauty we love is the brilliance of truth; and, as Sigmund Freud said, love is our relationship to beauty.

17. Jealousy is not Part of Love

Today, it appears to be self-evident that jealousy is a part of love. Jealousy is one of the basic paradigms of our time and is seen as a kind of psychological natural constant, in the belief that it is a part of human life, just as the thorn is a part of the rose. I do not know if there are roses without thorns, but I do know there is love without jealousy. It's the belief that we can have our beloved all to ourselves and "protect" him or her from access by others that results in the worldwide tragedy of a false doctrine of love. Jealousy is a false belief system. As long as humanity believes in jealousy, human beings will never be happy.

Jealousy is not part of love, for love is the dissolution of all jealousy. True love is connected to trust, and in the state of such trust, no relationship breaks up because of the sexual "infidelity" of a partner, whether male or female. Here, women tend to have the same general needs as men.

We want to and must create a world in which the sexual attention of one person to another does not result in jealousy, fear of abandonment or hatred in a third person.

This is a totally realistic goal. It is even a precondition for the emergence of a humane culture that at heart remains humane if someone is "unfaithful." Almost everyone who has sworn eternal faithfulness has at some time been "unfaithful." Let us stop deceiving ourselves about a kind of morality we cannot adhere to because it is not ours. Deep in our souls there is a different concept of love, which for so long has been waiting to be recognized and fulfilled.

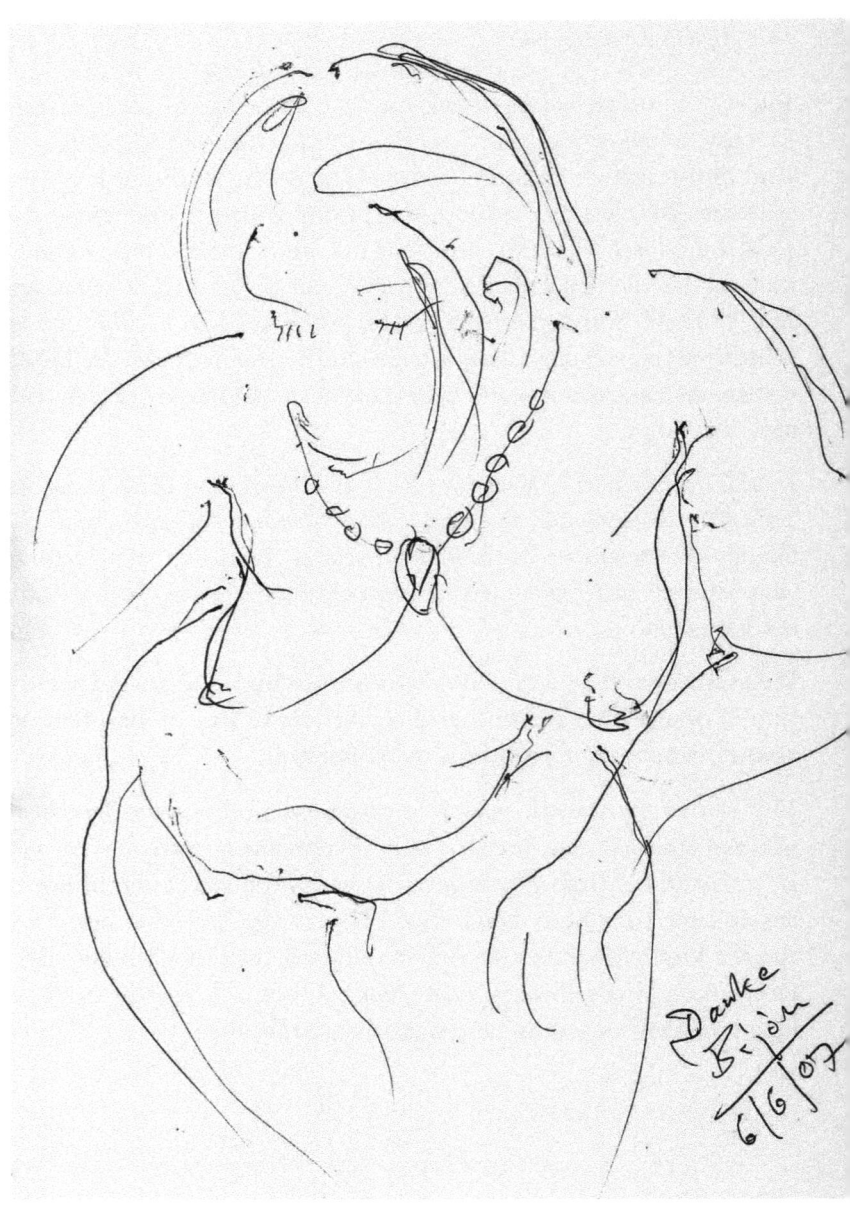

Thank You, Bijou, 2007

18. The Fisherman's Tear

In her book *Women Who Run with the Wolves,* Clarissa Estés tells a wonderful story about the fate of love. It is an old Inuit fable. The man is an Eskimo fisherman who fishes a woman, the emaciated skeleton of our primal nature, out of the water. While asleep, a tear runs down from the corner of the fisherman's eye. The skeleton-like woman crawls awkwardly to his side and slurps up the tear from his cheek like someone dying of thirst. She felt his sudden opening and compassion, through which he touched both her and his innermost nature. Now, something new can grow in him, something he can give as a gift to his life partner: a large, oceanic, feeling heart. Now the woman's primeval nature awakens and surrounds her skeleton with the living flesh of a loving woman.

What both of them are experiencing here can be applied to all of humanity. At some point the man awakes from his torpor, his unfulfillable projections and neediness, as well as from his disillusionments and hardened heart that he directs towards the woman. He now "recognizes" the woman and her (historic) fate; he weeps as he experiences a new kind of compassion and feels how he, too, has lost his primeval nature. Both of them are in a state of awakening from a joint hypnosis. The man, who for generations has simply co-existed next to the woman because he was too angry or too busy to "see" her, has himself become deeply miserable as a result of this alienation. By suppressing woman, the historical man could not recognize her true nature and thereby lost his own. Only by seeing the primeval nature of man and woman could both of them awaken from their hypnosis.

The primeval nature of humans also includes compassion with the fate of our co-creatures. Friedrich Nietzsche encountered this primeval nature when, one morning in 1889, he saw a horse being brutally flogged by its owner. Spontaneously, he flung his arms around its neck. After that he never spoke a word until he died in 1900. Compassion with a simple animal broke the heart of the creator of the great Zarathustra. Or did it rather open it? From then on, he was a different person.

When it comes to love, we need to recognize the ideological walls we have built around the entire topic of sex, love and partnership. We need to dismantle this wall and create new life forms in which both sexes can create new openings for each other.

In today's world, the concept of a "primeval nature" can be confusing. It assumes that there is something in the human being that connects them with the primal forces of life, in a sense with "God's primal force field." This primeval nature includes the core forces of sexuality and love, but also those of ethics and compassion. Many people who today are helping refugees are following an inner impulse from their ethical primeval nature. Our connection with our primeval nature lets us feel the fate of our co-creatures. Here, the great paradigm shift is being prepared that can be summarized with the encompassing word "Love." We experience our own primeval nature most directly in overt lovemaking between the sexes. What would a society look like in which this part of men and women would be celebrated, openly and freely, without claims of ownership and jealousy?

19. Arousal

Eros is a numinous power; it bombards us from within with a long-ing we can hardly escape. The arousal can become so strong that people lose control and satisfy their greed with violence, but the opposite can also occur: That we, in the most "decisive" moment, are no longer able to do "it." Sexual impotence often appears specifi-cally among those who are hit the hardest by the erotic power. The problem is not a lack of sexual energy, but the opposite: an excess of longing that cannot be fulfilled because it runs into an inner block-age that we have a hard time defining. Behind the word "shyness" there is often an enormous, nameless, inner turmoil. When I visited my first great love in Munich at the age of twenty, I sensed the ap-proaching sexual encounter, but I couldn't do it. For me she was a Goddess. Adoration and sex did not go together yet. We had another glass of wine and then I had to leave quickly. Anything else would have been too much for me. I then painted a picture that depicted our trembling excitement, which I called "Passing the wine glass." (See page 13)

I still remember the verses of a poem by Hugo von Hofmannsthal:

And yet when reaching for the hand
Which would this light cup have bestowed,
The burden proved for both too great,
For both, in trembling, knew a state
Where neither hand its partner found,
And so to earth the dark wine flowed.

Over the course of generations, a mutual projection has developed between the sexes that does not reflect current reality. Adoration and lust want to come together. For a long time there has been an arousal within the body of humanity. If no healthy valve can be found for it, only harm can come of it. This arousal heralds a coming pleasure and lust on both parts. We are standing at the gate of the "forbidden lust," the so-called "sin," which in church literature is often called "original sin," the sexual union of Adam and Eve, of man and woman. Today, we can understand the connections. We want to liberate Eros from all sin, without destroying the appeal that it had as sin.

20. Affirming Our Wild Sexual Nature

The French Jesuit Father Teilhard de Chardin gave us a surprising statement:

"The most vivid of tangible realities is the Flesh, and for Man, Flesh is Woman."

This, from the same man who wrote "The Eternal Feminine." What did he mean by this – and what do we associate it with today? What is the meaning of the "flesh" in the meeting of the sexes? "Flesh" is here a word for the innermost aspect of the body, its most naked and authentic movement in the state of lust, the "orgonotic primal pulsation" (Wilhelm Reich). It is one of the basic functions of life. In this state, the bodies of two lovers form an energetic union that is animated by the streams of healing, joy of life and of Creation. Is it not amazing that a Catholic Jesuit priest knew this?

Here is yet another quote from literary history, written by the German philosopher Arthur Schopenhauer:

"If I am asked where the most intimate knowledge of that inner essence of the world, of that thing in itself which I called the will to live, is to be found, or where that essence enters most clearly into our consciousness, or where it achieves the purest revelation of itself – then I must point to ecstasy in the act of copulation. That is it! That is the true essence and core of all things, the goal and the purpose of all existence." (From his book *The World as Will and Representation*)

Is it not amazing that a German philosopher knew this 200 years ago?

There can be no peace on Earth as long as there is war in love. There is especially one point in the relationship between the genders that determines if there will be war or peace on Earth. I mean the point of sexual desire and lust, where the body is loved and enjoyed in animalistic joy. "I love you so much I could eat you." Here, a high-tension current is flowing that can flood everything else – the passion of the flesh. Whether happiness or misery results from an "animalistic" union depends on the spirit in which it occurs. The magic word for happiness is "contact." Contact is a deep word, stemming from the Latin word "contingere" – it literally means "being connected." When two souls meet physically in this kind of contact, love arises – sexual love. That is the point where sex and love come together in the primal source of Eros.

This is the wild, lustful, irresistible power that so far has been banned from our cultural canon. In the name of truth and love, it must finally be accepted and affirmed. Happiness or misery in society also depends on to what extent it can find a positive attitude towards its own inner drives. As long as the wild side of Eros is repressed, it will continue to smolder underground, leading to uncontrolled eruptions. In our society, there is a sediment of sexual violence, of sadomasochism and fantasies of slaughter, that has so far led to terrible consequences in all wars. Everything that has been conceived of in sadistic masturbation fantasies or brutal comic strips has already been carried out at some time, somewhere. The revelations during the past few decades show that such barbarisms reach into the highest levels of society. The force field of suppressed sexuality contains a terrible longing for crossing boundaries, gaining perverse satisfaction and sexual violence. This longing is only waiting for a suitable opportunity. The entire history of wars can also be understood from this perspective.

Whenever humans try to suppress elementary forces, these forces sooner or later turn into violence, creating endless cruelty. This has been the case often enough in the history of the past millennia and is still happening worldwide today. Life energy is transformed into death energy. The victims are almost always women. Today, within the framework of global child pornography, innumerable children are also victims. There is a worldwide field of sexual violence on Earth. It is the result of an unspeakable transgression when channeling the sexual forces of life. If ever a true peace movement emerges it should no longer deplore the many sexual deviations, but instead find out how the Earth can be liberated from sexual violence. It thus needs to deal with an unusual topic.

The suppression of elementary sexual forces leads to further perversions that are committed, especially against animals. Animate and highly intelligent beings – cows and pigs are seen as "livestock" and raised for meat production. They are then prepared for human consumption in "slaughterhouses." In the collective unconscious of our pornographic society, the very concept of "meat" or "flesh"[2] has given rise to disastrous associations. Flesh no longer has to do with the idea of caressing, but with the notion of slaughter. This is true not only for animals. Does not slaughter have a tangible sexual component? Even as a child I felt sexual impulses when I saw how pigs were slaughtered. In the twisted brains of men, associations between women and pigs have been developed of which one hardly dares speak. If this collective and historic aberration had not occurred, we would have developed an entirely different attitude towards living flesh, an attitude of love and adoration, for flesh contains the entire miracle of life. I do not know if men who had gotten to love the flesh of woman would still be able to slaughter pigs.

Wild lust comes from the same divine source as love; it is a part of the sacred matrix. This power could not be acknowledged by the great religions; instead it was thrown in the gutter. We must pick it up from there, cleanse it from all prejudice and celebrate it in an appropriate way.

The acceptance of our wild nature, the acceptance of the lust of the flesh, and the acceptance of our divine animal nature is a prerequisite for a world without war.

If trust is established between the sexes, and if this trust reaches into the most intimate regions of lust, and if this process occurs not only briefly between two partners but becomes an integral part of a new

---

[2] Translator's note: In German, the word for "meat" is the same as for "flesh.

erotic culture, then something truly new will emerge. The hologram of fear will have then transformed into a hologram of trust. New neurotransmitters will then be produced in the body of humanity. It will hardly be physiologically possible to kill each other anymore.

The suppression and concealment of animal desires brought lies into the world that since then continue to operate in the form of a latent war between the sexes. The patriarchal fight against woman and the body has left behind deep scars in both women and men. Throughout the millennia it was not possible for a woman to reveal her primal sexual nature without risking losing her reputation or her life. To illustrate the primal nature with the words of others, I would again like to quote Clarissa Estés, from her book *Women Who Run with the Wolves*:

"Every woman carries a primal force within her that lies buried in the deepest, unexplored parts of her female psyche: her natural wildness, full of precise instincts, passionate power and ageless wisdom. This source of female primal energy now needs to be found by modern woman. ... We are all filled with a longing for the wild. There are few culturally sanctioned antidotes for this yearning. We were taught to feel shame for such a desire. We grew our hair long and used it to hide our feelings. But the shadow of Wild Woman still lurks behind us during our days and in our nights. No matter where we are, the shadow that trots behind us is definitely four-footed."

3/4/2004
DD, Bodega
(Die beste Zeichnung
an diesem Tag)

Bodega (The best drawing on this day), 2004

21. THE CALM IN THE EYE OF THE HURRICANE

Whereas the love life of the sexes used to be somewhat stabilized by the conventional rules of society, today it is totally out of balance. We live in chaotic times. Rings of unstoppable turbulence surround the Earth. They exist mentally, emotionally and spiritually within the individual as well as externally in politics. These two aspects are always connected. What happens externally impacts the interior of every individual, and what occurs inside always produces the external. Together, they today create an unparalleled global turmoil. The world is like a hurricane that drives us towards new boundaries. In a sense, we are all living at the edge. But we can also see the great secret of the hurricane: It rotates around a center, in which there is absolute stillness. It is the point of the highest energy. What kind of a mystery is that? What does this weather phenomenon tell us? To me it seems like a parable for our human situation. We are in the turbulent fields where the forces conflict, but we also see the eternal center, the point of stillness, power and procreation. Teilhard de Chardin called it "God's staging post" or the "Omega Point."

This point is a fact in the blueprint of Creation. All humans are connected with this point. The birth pangs of an emerging world are inevitably driving us towards it. We experience how our fears and aggressions dissolve at this point. It is truly a point of deepest peace; some people have experienced it while in a coma. Here, powerful transformational and healing forces are at work. Once we have arrived at this center, we recognize the meaning and purpose of our long journey. We now need staying power so as to understand what opportunities, what forces, what freedom and love want to be born here.

As I see it, the long-term force of survival of a love relationship or an entire community depends on to what extent they are able to create this high inner space among each other, to care for it and carry it into all areas of work. Here it gains cohesion and stability with which it can react adequately to the turbulence of our existence. Where and how we set our priorities is definitely a question of consciousness. No matter how we set them, unless we cultivate this quiet inner space, our efforts will fail due to the pressure of inner conflicts or outer "practical constraints." It is through the jointly experienced center that love and community attain their powers of regeneration, with which they can withstand the turbulence of our times.

22. The Rage of Woman

We have a daily "Forum" at our Tamera research station, in which people can go into the middle of the group and freely express their personal thoughts and emotions. As soon as full trust has been established between the participants, surprising things are revealed. This is especially the case for the rage of woman. Almost all women feel a numinous rage in the background of their lives; a rage they often cannot define. It is often discharged in irrational ways towards people who are close to them or towards their own love partner. Some women have looked deeply into their own rage. It almost always has to do with a deep disappointment in the area of sex, love and truthfulness. These are feelings of being deceived, of unfulfilled expectations and constant frustration. It is not much different for men, but they have other possibilities of compensating their rage through their profession, sports or power plays. Woman's rage is the result of a historical process, in which she had to suppress her own drives and her own nature.

King Cecrops, the mythical founder of Athens, introduced monogamy in Greece in the middle of the 2nd century B.C. Soon, all kingdoms adopted this model. Imagine what this meant for women, who came from a more or less pronounced matriarchal cultural tradition. They were now married to a man and had to stay with him their whole lives. In the beginning, they did not do this voluntarily. Harsh punishment was necessary to force them into this new fate. This is where the institutional suppression of woman began, in the name of male dominance. This story was then repeated by all religions. In the Old Testament, in Christianity and in the Koran, we find explicit reference to the legitimacy of man using violence against woman.

The women who today dream of marriage no longer know that this form of love was not initially a part of woman's nature, but had to be implemented with violence.

From then on, women lived under the yoke of men. Woman, who was full of sexual lust and wildness, had to submit to a law that was not hers. From then on, she lived in constant conflict, without being able to dissolve it: In the conflict between her animal and her Marian side, between the saint and the whore. Today, practically all women live in this conflict. As Goethe writes: "Two souls live in my breast ..." Only when both come together in harmony can love arise, a love of which we are all dreaming. Once we have seen and understood this, we gain an impression of what is happening today behind the scenes and of the joy that arises when these things are revealed and dissolved.

This is the first chapter of the historical rage of woman. But there is more: the man often refused her his sexual services. The initial fire of passion was soon extinguished and the river of sexual empathy turned into a trickle. Woman, who in social life hardly had any opportunity to gain fulfillment, now also found none in love and sexuality. This hit her at a sensitive spot, for sexual self-confidence is an essential part of the female identity. To understand this, we need a deeper understanding of the process that we so flippantly describe with the word "sexuality." It is a fundamental, biological, emotional and spiritual process of human life – for both sexes. When this process is hidden, suppressed or destroyed, it hits a central nerve in our human existence. As long as we have to remain silent about these connections, rage arises in the depths of almost every female soul. The result is compensation through consumption, church, gummy bears or extreme political positions. Such compensation leads to psychological and physical changes. The rage eats away at the body and the vicarious satisfaction bloats the flesh. You either become thin or fat. Almost all psychosomatic disruptions of our time are caused by the injury that our cultural tradition has inflicted on the free flow of sexual energies. Compare this with the beauty of women in a state of fulfilled sexuality and love.

23. Eros and Agape

In many people's minds, Eros is associated with an image of passion that does not quite fit with the idea of altruism. "Humaneness is not sexy." This is a disastrous image – a direct copy of a sexuality gone wrong. Sexual love and altruism, Eros and Agape, constitute a spiritual-emotional unit; both are a part of the primal human nature and both are an aspect of the sacred matrix. Just as the (nonviolent) opening of the animal nature is a quality of liberated love between the sexes, altruism is also a quality of liberated Eros.

Within the body-soul organism of the human being, there is a deep connection between the thinking organ, the sexual organ and the heart organ. When the energy flow from the sexual area meets up inside the heart with the energy flow from the head, the initial shining light image of the human being emerges. The old Egyptians called it the "Merkaba."

If this image is reinforced by a trusting community, the heart chakra takes on the central guiding function for the social, sexual and intellectual life. A flow of warmth arises for the mind and for Eros. No violence can exist if the heart guides human history.

I would like to repeat this last sentence: No violence can exist if the heart guides human history. Imagine for a moment a world of fulfilled Eros, a world without mistrust and fear in love. Once the experience of mutual trust has created a human foundation, the ethics of altruism will automatically arise. A heart that no longer suffers under the constant stress of unfulfilled needs is free for others. The healing of inner conflicts opens up a loving relationship with all fellow humans and fellow creatures. If two women love the same man, they will not fight each other; instead, they will bond deeply. We have experienced this, again and again in Tamera. Sexual love without competition and jealousy truly exists. Women love to mutually support each other in this regard. Compassion, a willingness to help and altruism are natural functions in people who are no longer in conflict with themselves. If one is free of this inner fight, one cannot condemn others. The power that has liberated oneself now wants to help others. A fulfilled Eros carries a permanent vibration for loving compassion towards the life of others. One wants to and has to share the fullness that one has partaken of. These are simple and elementary connections in the world order of the sacred matrix that are immediately reflected within ourselves as soon as we are connected with this order.

24. TRANSSEXUALITY

Most people are either male or female; they have an unambiguous sexual identity. I do not know who ultimately makes the decision regarding our sexual identity. It seems as if, even before we were born, we wrote a script for our coming incarnation in which we made a decision for one side or the other.

In the following, I will assume that the concept of reincarnation is true, as has repeatedly been indicated in "regression trances" (by professional reincarnation researchers). In such regressions we have experienced that the sexual identity of a being is not set in stone once and for all, but can change from one incarnation to the next. Someone who is a woman today can previously have been a man and the other way around. In the course of our karmic biography, we truly go through such changes because we need to experience what the world feels like in a female body and in the body of a man. In the case of transsexuality – perhaps on purpose and for good reasons – either no decision has been made or a decision in a different direction has been made.

In this connection I wish to refer to the striking story of the young American whistleblower Bradley Manning. Manning was a very courageous person, who no longer wanted to be a part of the lies and deceit around the war in Iraq. So he published exposés on the internet. A court sentenced him to lifelong imprisonment for betraying state secrets until he was pardoned by Obama a few years later. In prison, Manning underwent an operation that turned him into a woman. What goes on in a person who makes such a decision? It is clear that we are here dealing with one of the deepest issues that affect not only private individuals, but in principle all of humanity: an existential reevaluation of the sexual role one has taken on and the courage to express a truth beyond all roles. It can be an inspiration for many to again fundamentally reconsider the roles they play.

We live in a time of a lack of overall sexual orientation. There are good reasons for this. Too many bad things have been done in the name of the old role patterns, and the walls that "normal" people have erected against those who are "abnormal" have been too terrible. Against this background it is understandable that lives are chosen outside of fixed sexual allocations and the corresponding role patterns. I do not think this is an evolutionary error but a pause to open up to new possibilities. Transsexuals are a serious challenge for all of us to rethink the entire topic of our sexual identity. The old polarities are being dissolved and new ones are not yet visible. And still, behind all these facts, we have the polarity between man and woman which cannot be abolished, either by future visions of androgynous people or through unisex or cybersex. The future will show what will develop in human society when this basic fact has been understood. We live in a world of becoming, with many openings up ahead.

25. FREE SEXUALITY AND PARTNERSHIP

*You can only be faithful, if you're allowed
to love others, too.*

First, I want to explain what is meant by free sexuality. It is a question of truth and trust in the relationship between the sexes, and especially of truth in the area of sexual desire. It is not about indiscriminate promiscuity and uncommitted relationships. It is about lovers not lying to each other, even if they are together with others. This is an ethical imperative. We cannot realize free sexuality as long as someone has to be lied to. There are ethical rules that do not allow it. The culture of free sexuality is firmly connected with these rules. We know of the anguish of a partner who has to conceal his or her sexual relationship towards another person. It is cruel for all those affected and for the children.

Earlier in life, when I was in love, I was always only in love with one person. That happened often in my life. If someone would have told me, while in the state of such infatuation, about free sexuality, I would have regarded him as somewhat crazy. I might even have been indignant. I didn't want to have anything to do with such a weird ideology.

But free sexuality is not an ideology; it is an aid in gaining sexual honesty – a possibility to deal honestly with our sexual inclinations. It is important that the experience occurs in a social and ethical environment of trust. Nobody should be compelled to practice free sexuality; that must be absolutely clear. But if lovers notice that one or both partners would like to open up to others, this should not be a reason for concealment, lies or separation. Free sexuality only means sexuality without fear, hypocrisy and lies – and ultimately without jealousy! Jealousy is the source of terrible things. Children often sense that they can no longer trust their parents. A society whose members live in such unstable love relationships is built on sand.

Free sexuality is tied to three principles without which it can never work: contact, trust and solidarity. In order for man and woman to become truthful regarding their respective longings and to no longer have to cheat secretly, they need contact, trust and solidarity. That is a lot. Contact means that we see the soul of the other person and not only their body. Trust means that we no longer lie to each other. Solidarity means that man and woman interact with each other in solidarity, true friendship and cooperation, without judgment or irony. In the existing world, these preconditions are usually not fulfilled. We thus have to create new systems in which it again becomes possible to orient our lives towards basic human values. We need a system of human co-existence in which people can trust each other again – a system in which lies and falseness no longer provide an evolutionary advantage, a system in which the sexual relationship between two people no longer triggers fear and hatred in a third person.

How do we solve the seeming contradiction between free love and couple love, between free sexuality and partnership? This constitutes a real problem because we humans not only want free sexuality, we also want a stable and permanent partnership "until death do us part." Suddenly, we are faced with a seemingly unsolvable conflict: the conflict between the new image of free sexuality and the old marriage archetype. The archetypal image of marriage, the eternal relationship between one man and one woman, is deeply rooted in the human soul. We all know it, and we all have a longing in this direction. Every longing is waiting for its fulfillment; we would not have any longing if there were no corresponding fulfillment, for our longings are not random. If a community is fully focused on free sexuality and thereby ignores this deep longing, it is bound to fail. Here, we can use Hegel's dialectic theory: thesis – antithesis – synthesis. The thesis is marriage. The antithesis is free sexuality. The synthesis is a new system, in which the thesis and the antithesis are integrated and united at a higher level. We have been working for a few decades to find this synthesis.

Many people who have gone through thick and thin in this project and have stayed now sense the existence of this "third way," and the real possibility of winning one without losing the other. Slowly, they understand the statement that was made at the beginning of the project and has been repeated at all our events: Free sexuality and partnership do not exclude each other; they complement each other. Whoever lives in a permanent relationship does not have to fear losing their partner because of other sexual contacts, and whoever lives in free sexuality does not have to fear missing out on the joy of a permanent partnership. All these conflicts exist only in our heads, not in the logic of things. For both – marriage and free sexuality – complement each other. They belong together, and together they form the essence of a new erotic culture. But they only fit together under certain social and ethical preconditions. The seeming contradiction between free sexuality and sexuality between two people exclusively can only be resolved at a higher level of order.

What is the higher level of order? In one word, it is the level of trust. As long as there is mistrust between the sexes, the contradiction cannot be resolved. As soon as real trust arises, it is already resolved, for it is natural that both partners once in a while are attracted to others, and it is also natural for a true love relationship not to break down because of it. I wish that all couples who come to Tamera from far away find and understand this naturalness. Jealousy is not a part of love. It takes a while for us to liberate ourselves from the old conditionings, and yet it went fairly quickly for most co-workers. If both sexes feel fully free to acknowledge their polygamous delights, they can build their partnership equally freely, for they have eliminated secret mistrust. If they no longer react with jealousy to their partner's occasional affairs, their sexual love of each other begins to grow in a new way. If one of them is caught up in a conflict, we can only tell them: Follow love!

"Free sexuality" is a cultural concept, not a masturbation fantasy. Sexual liberation does not solve the entire gender issue, but we have then removed an inner blockage and can continue on the path of love and trust.

To create trust between the sexes, we need a life order that makes a free, honest sexual life possible.

Pornographic obsessions of violence and submission usually dissolve by themselves in a field of liberated sexuality in which we have learned to live in full contact with each other.

"Free sexuality" was a key concept in the great revolt of 1968. We needed this concept to combine the thoughts of external revolution with an inner revolution. But we could not yet attain this emancipatory goal, because we could not yet see what inner, ethical and emotional-spiritual preconditions have to be fulfilled to be able to live a truly humane and liberated sexual life. Sexual liberation failed due to the inner powers of domination, competition and jealousy. When the movement fell apart, most comrades returned to their private spheres and had love relationships and marriages like everyone else. I experienced free sexuality a second time at Friedrichshof in Austria in the 70s, where the artist Otto Mühl had established an unusual community with the key concept of "free sexuality." I was impressed by the radicality of this experiment, but I soon saw its inhuman dogmatism and had confrontations with the founder that made any cooperation impossible. But from then on, I knew that there was no getting around the truth of free sexuality; however, it needed a different ethical and spiritual foundation.

The culture of free sexuality is a culture without lies, humiliation and violence. It can only function on a solid foundation of trust. The sexes learn to let go of old prejudices and projections and enter into a partner relationship that is on an absolutely equal footing. They meet as equals. This is no formal "gender equality" and no equalization. Instead it is the insight into a blueprint of life, where the feminine and the masculine must balance each other without any false harmony for the whole to be able to function harmoniously. The union of opposites ("coincidentia oppositorum") can only occur when the two poles meet and connect with the same power. Knowledge about this law is not derived from books, but from a life practice and an ethic that no longer allows for subordination or domination. The emancipation of women goes hand in hand with the emancipation of men and vice versa. It was surprising to see with what liberation and joy most women entered into free sexuality and continue to do so. For many men it was not an easy experience to see how happy their partners were to engage with others sexually. The sexual emancipation of women places immediate demands on the emancipation of men, especially on his ability to make contact.

Being happy or unhappy is a question of contact. Free sexuality without this special loving contact does not contribute much to happiness. It needs trusting contact as a foundation. The new culture is neither patriarchal nor matriarchal, but based on partnership.

26. Don't Leave

There is hardly a deeper request than this. It shows how much two lovers need each other, often especially in situations of conflict. Is perhaps the primal fear of separation at the core of all our fears?

The history of love is also a history of separation anxiety. This fear is connected with an unspeakable fate. "Please don't leave" – what is happening the moment this plea is spoken is a part of the daily drama of the world and everyone understands it immediately. There is much at stake here, both for one's own person and for the children. It is as if one were to lose the foundation of one's own life. And then it actually happens!

I read in the paper about the death of a young pair of lovers. They had tied themselves to each other and jumped off a cliff. One can understand the logic of this act: They wanted to remain together forever and they wanted to be absolutely certain of their eternal faithfulness, but they sensed the challenges they would face in the world and they avoided all dangers by choosing death together. It's a true story. This is how deep the desire of the sexes is to be together forever. And this is how deep the pain is when a relationship breaks up. But this happens thousands of times every day on Earth. What happens to the children then?

There is a special tragedy in the fear of losing a partner: It is a fear that makes people do anything, cling to a person, threaten, beg to keep the beloved partner – and this very fear makes them actually lose him or her. We experience this drama everywhere and it can hardly be overcome through individual advice. The only thing that defends us against this recurring tragedy is an openness and a fullness in love that liberates us from all clinging and fixations, making it possible for people to remain together forever. It may seem like a paradox, and yet it is true: The certainty of keeping a partner comes about through the ability to let them go at any moment. That is what lovers do anyway, once they have discovered the law of love.

It has always been a goal of ours to lessen the fear of separation and replace it with the confidence of creating a firm human sense of belonging. The faithfulness between lovers or spouses grows by being embedded into the faithfulness of a community. That was the importance of earlier tribes. We want to create a new firm human basis for this, at a new historical level. It is a basis for all people who no longer need the old kind of walls around themselves for their inner cohesion.

27. A Home for the Children

A whole world needs whole children. Children need the security of a stable home of adults where they can grow up without the fear of separation and deceit. For such a home to exist, we need not only the two parents but also a stable community. The nuclear family is then socially embedded into a "community of the second order." Then others have no problem taking care of the children. It is really amazing how easy this has been in our community, right from the start. The children are then not so exclusively fixated on their parents; they establish intimate relationships with other adults as well. If one parent is not there, then the child spontaneously seeks out a replacement mother or father.

Children who grow up without a definable family are usually at some point interested in knowing who their biological parents are. Who is really my mother and who is my father? There seems to be a (karmic) relationship between a child and its parents that goes beyond the biological connection. Stable relationships between children and their parents are therefore desirable, also within the framework of communities with free love. But the generous way small children have of finding replacement parents within a free community is so amazing and convincing that we cannot give the question of the biological parents quite the same importance as has been the norm in the family mythology of the patriarchal culture.

Under the life conditions of our society it is by no means obvious for parents to love their children. They are often so occupied with their own problems that they see their children as a burden. Innumerable children become victims of broken marriages. The community of the second order consists of people who trust each other because they have learned the rules of living together and because they no longer have to hide themselves sexually. When adults no longer have to lie, a basis of trust arises in the community, making it possible for the parents to establish a loving relationship with each other and with their children. When parents participate in the lives of their chil-

Olivenbaum bei Torrão,
~ 2000 Jahre alt ~ gepflanzt zur Zeit von Jesus.
Hat die ganze Kirchengeschichte überlebt!

16/11/2015

Olive tree in Torrão, 2015

dren, they get to know the wonderful life processes through which they themselves can become young again.

Raising children freely was one of the goals that we wanted to attain fifty years ago through an "anti-authoritarian" education, but could not achieve, for every child needs a positive authority that it can lean on and trust. The tragedy of the children who grew up under the conditions of the anti-authoritarian movement was not that their parents had exercised too much authority, but that they either had no authority or did not want to take any on. The children thus grew up without orientation in a world without orientation. It is and remains the responsibility of the parents to provide trustworthy orientation for their children by being role models for them.

True authority is based on trust.

Children are cosmic beings who have come to Earth. Have we ever observed the alertness with which children look out into the world, even just a few days after being born? Have we let ourselves be touched and shaken by the attention of their large eyes? Have we felt the total presence of this spirit that is gazing out into this world? This is the first quality that children have that we must care for and protect: an absolute presence that is not clouded by fear or caution, their spiritual power of perception, their curiosity, awe and recognition. Right from the start the child is a perceiving and trusting being, and where this quality is recognized and supported by adults, the child has a spiritual home that determines their continued mental-spiritual development.

To love a child means to recognize it and support it joyfully. This is true for any love of another person. The child then does not need any further proof of love, for it is not in fear of neglect or separation. To no longer fear separation deep inside may be the foundation for every true feeling of home.

All our experiences tell us that, in a well-organized culture of free love, the relationships between the parents, as well as all human relationships, are substantially more stable than under the conditions of a regular marriage. There is no subliminal distrust, lying or deception between the partners. They now have a more stable foundation for their longing to be together in a family. Nobody will jump ship because of jealousy. Slowly but surely, a spiritual humus layer has formed in the community, in which occasional aggressions can land smoothly. A natural, social ethic has been created that leaves no one behind.

It is with amazement that we on a daily basis experience how such a social climate rubs off on the children. It is moving to see how they take care of each other and the friendliness with which they react to each other. They are wild like all children, but they don't beat each other; they don't get into competitive fights; they do not betray each other or snitch on each other to the adults; they learn fast; they develop their own children's theater; they learn Portuguese and perform their theater in Portuguese; they develop enormous acrobatic abilities in the gym and they clearly let you know if something is not to their liking. Even if it isn't all ideal, our children give us deep insights about the inner powers and possibilities of life, provided it is not blocked by prejudice.

28. A New Women's Field

Due to male dominance in patriarchal society, the historic role of women was reduced to the bourgeois model of the three Cs: Cooking, Children and Church. Although these are, without a doubt, key areas at the heart of every community, this constriction did not let woman draw on her original source of power. If we elevate the CCC model to encompass a larger view, an entirely different image emerges. The women will take on leadership positions in all areas in which the foundations of life are built anew, i.e. in all social, ecological and political areas of a life-oriented culture. They will again open their own sources and slowly but surely let go of the old concepts of life that told them that it is imperative that they have a man at their side.

I know and understand the longing of many women for "the" man. Who does not understand it? Just as sons are tied to their mothers, daughters are also connected with their fathers with a natural love and therefore hold a beloved father imago in their hearts. Here, we have an opening in love that needs to remain open in the new world, too. The error occurs when this bond with the high image of men becomes an overpowering spiritual and erotic fixation. For in addition to men, woman has a different source of life: her deep connection to the elementary nature of life and all living creatures. This connection lies outside of all relationship issues, and in an organic society it cannot be replaced by a love relationship with a single man. The polarity of the genders does not consist of a woman being dependent on a man or – as a feminist countermovement – fighting men, but of her taking her great place in Creation again. When a woman becomes small in love, she is misunderstanding her own role. If a woman chases after a man, she is probably not in harmony with evolution.

Seen from a distance, this all seems like a strange occurrence, because due to her archetypal form and function, the woman is the guiding force regarding the basic issues of life and love. Her evolutionary role and her deep connection with life give her a different authority and universality than that of simply being the partner or spouse of a man. If a woman uses the power of her female instincts to tie a single man to herself, she will probably at some point either wither from sexual frustration or else suffocate this man with her motherliness. In both cases this inner excess of power, which is a part of her universal nature, could not be accommodated. No woman can unfold the divine gift of sex, love, care and intelligence that Creation has given her in a relationship with a single man. Her sexual, social and intellectual nature point towards a higher social purpose. The man has the task to help her and, in a sense, "to be there for her," just as the reverse used to hold true. The man is a "fueling station" for the woman, but he cannot claim her for himself alone. And yet this absolute love between a man and a woman does exist, as I described in Chapter 16. The woman's change of roles does not contradict the spiritual power of eternal love.

When women again accept their larger role, they automatically become active forces of an emerging emancipatory community. They live, think and work based on a common source within the framework of a large common goal. They will no longer fight each other when it comes to men. In Tamera we have often enough seen the effects of true solidarity between women in this area. Some simple examples: A woman desires a man, but he is together with her girlfriend. The girlfriend understands her friend's wish and offers her her apartment for the night. For she knows that her man is attractive also to other women – and she also knows that no friendship will end because of it.

We are dealing with a historic change of roles for today's woman that is at the heart of a new gender order. Many women today notice that their development has to go in this direction. They no longer see the possibility of finding the "strong man" in whose arms they can stay small. They themselves must help create men whom they want to give themselves to. They are a guiding force in the area of love, whether they want to be or not, and the greatest service they can give to any community is to decide to take on this role.

The creation of a new women's field constitutes a new level in the evolution of humanity and in the evolution of life on Earth. If the female natural force is liberated from thinking in terms of relationship, then all forces of love tend to be liberated from thinking in terms of relationship. The new field has to do with such a central aspect of life that all things are affected by it; nutrition, natural science, ecology, cooperation with animals, raising children, and so on will all have a different meaning afterwards than they did before. Children will grow up within a human framework that is no longer dependent on the moods of two parents. Youths will receive an introduction to sexuality that spares them many wrong turns and much deception, and the men will notice that in addition to their profession and "practical constraints," there is something wonderful that it pays to live for.

29. THE END OF THE WAR BETWEEN THE GENDERS AND SEXUAL VIOLENCE

Imagine Moses going up on Mount Sinai a second time. There he meets a wonderful woman and experiences the erotic bliss that all people have always been seeking. Because as a man he is systematic, he writes down his experience in the form of ten new statements. They are no longer the Ten Commandments of old, but ten basic rules of a social and sexual ethic that comes from love. Here, there are other "commandments" than the imperatives that begin with "Thou shalt" or "Thou shalt not." Here, we find the basic rules of compassion, truth, love and joy. It is a wonderful message. All people can hear and understand it.

Let us imagine that these words have the same power as the words in the Ten Commandments from back then and that they spread around the world. The new Moses would have received them from the mouth of a woman. She spoke to him just as the Sphinx raises her voice above the great Pyramids during the annual festival at Giza. The entire human race turns its head to read these new tablets of life. A new field of information then emerges for a new cultural development.

Every human culture is rooted in a canon of values that are passed on from generation to generation and turn into a collective guiding system, which determines the behavior of humans. This gives rise to the "morphogenetic fields" of human history that guide how humanity develops. If they produce humane or cruel societies; if their participants suffer from the fear of abandonment or live together in trust with each other; what they regard as possible or impossible – all this largely depends on the basic information humanity follows. The goal of our work, the goal of the global Healing Biotopes plan, is to replace the old information field of domination and submission, fear and violence, that for millennia has led humanity down a dead end street, with a new information field of trust, solidarity and co-operation with all beings.

When we succeed in revealing to each other the original love between man and woman in a trusting encounter, when we have created a social ethic in which there is no deception and no humiliation, and when the first communities are able to dissolve the historical trauma, then we will live in a world in which there can no longer be a war between the sexes nor any sexual violence. The old pattern of lies and deceit, suspicion and secrecy will then be a thing of the past. When the hearts that once had to close themselves off begin to open again, when this flow of warmth guides our contacts, our organism switches automatically from the old matrix of fear to the new matrix of love. No man could ever again raise his hand against a woman and no woman would have to fear being betrayed or raped. For in this new world, betrayal and violence no longer have a source that feeds it. A society that has disentangled itself from the legacy of its cruel past automatically transforms into a society of love, for love is the raw material of life. The natural state in which the sexes are connected with each other is called love.

30. Defend the Sacred

Elementary values such as truth, trust, courage, solidarity, mutual support, love and compassion are a part of the sacred matrix. The concept of the new centers includes entrenching these values so deeply that they can no longer be destroyed.

"Defend the Sacred." That was the motto of the Indigenous activists at Standing Rock in the US, in the movement to protect their land from the pipelines of the oil companies. We have for some time been living in a personal and spiritual connection with their leaders. Today, "Defend the Sacred" is turning into a global movement in which we cooperate with the leaders of Standing Rock as well as with other Indigenous leaders and peace activists from around the world to initiate a system change. Life must be defended everywhere against the established powers. Water and love are among the most sacred things in life. Water is for nature what love is for human beings.

Including love in the cycles of nature creates a different frequency in the hologram of life. Animals then seek contact with humans because they no longer have to fear them, and humans lose their old fear of snakes, spiders and other monsters, for they, too, are ciphers in the alphabet of life. All beings are part of a collective co-evolution, the great musical score in a joint vibration of life. We see or sense the spiritual dimension of a universe that radiates from within to its outermost emanations with the light of the eternal Sun that is forever reflected in every being. We recognize the real epiphany of a sacred world in all things that we so far simply passed by. It is a process of slow insight and increasing discovery, which step by step and portal by portal removes the walls that have so far separated us from the center of the unity. This is where the new power arises that is stronger than all violence. Here, where the world opens and communes, we find the primal experience of trust. We all have a (subconscious) memory of this experience and we have all forgotten it during our disastrous history. But when it returns, we all experience it as an intimately familiar déjà vu. "Oh, so it really does exist! So that was how it all was meant to be! It wasn't just a dream!" Whenever the reality of the sacred matrix reveals itself in this way among people, a new love emerges, which rises above all private love stories. This is the new power that changes our planet.

The transition from the hologram of violence to the hologram of peace is not only a question of an individual transformation from fear to trust; instead, it entails replacing a historical field of war with a morphogenetic field of peace. It is the opening of a gateway of humanity that in the past was so cruelly closed. It is a goal of the current transformation to open this gateway for all beings. The inner setting for this historic process lies in the global heart of an awakening humanity.

Whenever a group of committed people enters the spiritual flow of this stream of the world, either through studies or through community and new experiences of trust, a new force field of the new culture arises. There, a new code is written that spreads on Earth because it is in resonance with the deepest of life programs that are written into all participants of our universe: the resonance with the force field of the sacred matrix and its ethical rules. When men and women come together in this sense, the truth of love and loyalty arise, as does true solidarity and cooperation, the organizational forms of a new social order, and the decentralized systems of ecology and technology to provide energy, water and food. Here, ecological communities of a new kind arise globally: both Healing Biotopes and the network for a new Earth.

We are working and praying for this goal. May humanity no longer have to hope for salvation because it has found its home on this Earth.

In the name of love.
In the name of the children.
In the name of all beings.

PART II

Sabine Lichtenfels

THE FEMALE VOICE AND THE GATEWAY TO FORBIDDEN LUST

Symbol of the female power of the Goddess Isis in the stone circle of Tamera, designed and chiseled by Sabine Lichtenfels

Chapter 1: The Forbidden Gateway and Its Opening

The Female Voice

I am the eternal female. Everything is born of me and everything returns to me. I am the origin of all cultures. Men and women have worshiped me as the Great Mother. I was Inanna, Ishtar, Isis, Artemis, Yemaya and, time and again, Maria.

Something drove me from one incarnation to the next. It was the great longing for my counterpart, man. I have loved him so much, with my body, arms, legs, breasts and lips! I wanted to love everything of him that was alive – his skin, his hair – everything! Why was that so forbidden? Specifically, why did the greatest longing lead to the greatest catastrophes?

As Lilith, I was Adam's first wife and I was condemned for my sexual nature. As Eve, I spoke with the serpent and desired knowledge. Through me, sin came into the world. As Rahab, I became a traitor – out of love. As Eloise, I burned with longing – and unintentionally brought disaster to my lover. My longing and my beauty broke apart families and marriages. Armies and peoples were incited against each other – all because of me. As Mary Magdalene, I was very close to my goal – and yet I lost everything.

I am the eternal female, and I am of a deeply sexual nature. Man has always misunderstood me; he has desired, damned and punished me – and yet he could never forget me. Since he could not possess me, he wanted to destroy or forbid me. But I can never be totally destroyed. Whenever I am not welcome by day, I come by night – as a curse, as temptation and doom. But it is not the darkness itself that is evil; it only becomes evil by being excluded.

I live in the adulteress who is stoned and in the philosopher who is burned at the stake. I live in the despised whore who takes in the needy. I live in the nurse who untiringly cares for the ill and the injured, because care is the expression of her love. And I live in the researcher who gains precise knowledge about the world through her intimate contact with everything that lives.

They tried to domesticate me. They reduced my sphere of action so I couldn't breathe any more. They took away my voice. I almost lost consciousness – almost forgot who I was. Since my love was met with betrayal and oppression, century after century, I began to protect myself. I hid and became evil.

But this, too, has passed. The time has come for me to be reborn – in more and more women who find their source. The time has come to let it be known that we want to, and we can again, reach out to men on our joint path towards liberation from pain. The time has come for me to resurrect – as a love teacher, a woman of solidarity, a wise woman, a mother, a lover and a revolutionary. The time has come; let us do all this now, so that the sexes can wed as equally strong forces and poles of life.

THE FORBIDDEN GATEWAY – HOW COULD IT COME TO THIS?

The sky leans under the earth.
The earth lets mountains grow.
The heart embraces the earth.
The power protects the heart.

~ A prayer from a Native American altar ritual to balance the sky and the earth, power and love, man and woman

I would like to say, very simply, what touches me about peace. What is peace anyway? And what role does sexuality play in creating global peace? Have any words ever been invented for a form of peace that is more than ascetic, shallow and boring – a peace that doesn't heroically renounce desire, lust and sensuality?

Many religions assign true peace to the hereafter. But if peace cannot be found in this world, then why were we even born? Only to experience hell on Earth? Or can we activate soul images that unite lust and peace?

Images in which peace is tremendous, powerful and thrilling, fulfilling us and making us happy? Images in which lovers embrace without it ending in a drama of jealousy? Images in which Eros becomes a sacred fire and all life on this Earth becomes a mirror of the erotic process of creation?

How did sexuality – originally something sacred – become something vulgar? Why is there hardly anything in the sacred books about the fundamental, biological facts of life? Where are the words of the wise about the beauty, fullness, magnificence and depth of sensual reality? Why are there so few glorifications of the female aspects of divine fullness? Why did Jesus Christ have to be birthed by a virgin? How could the evangelists ignore the most sacred and elementary lustful beauty of the lovers' embrace, from which all life emerges?

The negation of sexuality and the suppression of the female began with the biblical story of the Fall. The expulsion from Paradise overshadows the history of humanity. But how did it come to this?

FROM THE RELIGION OF THE GREAT MOTHER TO THE PATRIARCHAL GOD

Originally, religion was a celebration of Creation, a thanksgiving to all life. The Great Mother was worshiped everywhere: in Sumer, Babylon, Mesopotamia, Crete and Old Egypt before the dynasties. Woman holds a great secret, the miracle of birth. She carries a child in her body for nine months, gives birth to it and has milk to feed it. She is the loving source for every newborn child. Is she not the Goddess herself – not only for every newborn child, but for all human beings?

The female was thus worshiped as the source that gives life. The Great Mother was totally physical. She was sometimes depicted as a voluptuous woman, sometimes in the form of a fish, a pig, a goat, a toad, a cow or a mare. She was the keeper of all life, the guardian over life and death, the essence of beauty and sensual love, and the gateway to sexual fulfillment.

Woman was thus paradise on Earth for every open male heart. There was not yet a taboo that banished sexual joy. The first human beings lived in this bliss of Creation. Legend calls them Adam and Eve. As a woman, Eve spoke to all the plants and animals, including the serpent, the great healing power of life. On its recommendation, she ate from the tree of knowledge. She convinced Adam to do the same and so seduced him into the realm of sensual joy.

"And Adam knew Eve, his wife; and she conceived…" it says in Genesis 4:1. Luther translated the word "yada" in the Hebrew original as "know." The same word was used for knowledge and sexuality.

But then something happened that is still incomprehensible today. The most beautiful thing – sensual love between the sexes – was declared to be evil. It was said that Adam and Eve had sinned, and that the future of all humanity was poisoned by their act. Because of her sexual nature, Eve was seen as more devilish than the devil, and together with Eve, the entire female gender was damned. Moreover, the serpent, together with everything of an animal nature, was banished. God cast out Adam and Eve from the Paradise of connectedness into the world of separation, enmity and scarcity. It was the beginning of a long, traumatic history for the human being. War became the father of all things.

But who did this? Who had such power? What Lord suddenly emerged in Heaven who did not want his children to love each other and know each other sensually? This was no longer a loving God; this was the jealous and punishing God of patriarchy. All patriarchal religions have one thing in common: The fight against lust and the submission of woman.

THE FIGHT AGAINST THE BODY AND AGAINST WOMAN

Woman and man had loved and desired each other deeply in trust and lust. So how did the loving companion become the avenging warrior, the punishing ruler? How did the female lover become the avenging fury, the dragon? What hit them so terribly that they had to close off their hearts and fight each other? What happened, especially to man, so that he lost his source and his trust in women? We are closing in on an answer: Sexuality, which initially was a source of pure joy, his own longing, had become so overpowering that he experienced it as threatening and had to fight and conquer it. And sexuality was embodied by the female gender. Woman must have experienced something similar. Her longing for a male partner who would be able to satisfy her desire was so immense that she demanded more strength from him than he was able to muster at this point in his evolutionary development.

In his misery, man discovered a different kind of power. It was no longer the power that comes from being embedded in Creation and its laws, the power of the open heart and contact. It was his own power, that resulted from separation. He hoped it would give him power over woman and over the Earth. It was the path of the closed heart. It made him cold and gave him the power of a warrior, and even sexual potency. Instead of becoming the woman's partner, he subjugated her. The patriarchal, punishing God was an invention of humans – especially male humans – who had lost their source and their trust in Creation.

The desire for power initiated the imperialist age. It declared what originally was strong to be weak, and what was weak to be strong. It was the representatives of the new monotheistic religions – Nietzsche described them as priests who had been eaten away by envy – who turned men and women alike away from the beauty of sensual love. They distorted the truth and could thereby rule. This broke the power of woman, her sexual abundance and authority. The body and the Earth became soulless objects that one could dominate and use. Tribes were exterminated, the Mother Goddesses and her rituals were prohibited, and new belief systems were violently forced onto people. Everything that was primordial, wild and elementary was banished to hell, to the darkness, to the world of subconscious and dangerous urges.

And the women? Why did they, who initially had such great social, spiritual and sexual power, put up with these developments? Why did they allow the men to have their way? Why did they acquiesce? Why did they not put up more effective resistance?

We can only assume that women's sexual longing for the strong man was so great that they began to act against their own interests. They put up with a lot; they bent over backwards to give the men space; and yes, many of them served men and became a part of the new system of destruction.

The God thus lost the Goddess next to him. It must have gotten lonely around him without his loving partner.

Primal Love

Eros is the origin, the deep source from which creation always occurs anew. The masculine and the feminine are expressions of the polar forces of the world, which bring forth all life. At heart, the entire process of creation is an erotic act of love. The Earth emerged from a procreative process of the male and female aspects of the world – one could say of God and Goddess. Life is the child of their love. The male aspect wants to enter ever deeper into the body, into matter, and the female wants to be lovingly known and penetrated. In the center, they are one unit.

Woman – the female in us – is directly connected with the physical, with matter. She lets her body speak – for her it is the temple of the mind – in how she moves, how she lingers close to a plant, suddenly understanding its essence. It is a high state of presence. In her essence, woman simply wants to love. She always wants to communicate; her entire being is oriented towards cooperation. In this space there is no violence and no enmity, no fear and no reason to protect oneself. There is only contact.

Man – the male in us – wants to comprehend by thinking, to actively grasp and understand. Man has his anchor in the metaphysical, the mental-spiritual area. It's from there that he approaches the material, the flesh, the female. If this process is allowed to occur without interruption, there is peace, and then "religio" occurs: a return to our sources, the religion of connectedness.

All our true love relationships are part of this primal, cosmic process. The whole is mirrored in every true sensual love relationship, and integration into the universally sensual process of creation is what will allow a new erotic culture to bloom.

There is a level at which the answer to all the misery of our times is very simple. It is an answer that ends all wars: We need liberation from the hypnosis of the patriarchal era and initiation into the fundamental facts of life.

SEXUALITY IN THE TIME OF EXPULSION

The condemnation of sexuality was the beginning of a unique historical process that turned all values upside down. Laws, scrolls and sermons drove home a feeling of guilt in humanity – for woman, because she was physical by nature, and for man because he was under her spell. Women were cruelly punished for revealing their sexual lust. Nobody was to enter the free land of sexual love in its pure beauty and power.

As long as we do not open the door to free, knowing sexuality, we live in the era of expulsion. Those who still have wealth and a physical home experience the homelessness of the soul. There is no haven of peace any more on this Earth. The inner and outer world of humans has been devastated and destroyed. We no longer know the experience of true home. A hypnotic spell determines all behavior patterns much faster than any thought: It is the belief that love is connected to suffering and pain. Free lust and love between partners have become contradictory. Those who choose partnership must rein in their lust. Those who choose lust destroy partnerships – and run headlong into disaster.

Consumption, wealth and prestige have become the gods of modern times. In order to climb up the career ladder, women have become more male than men. They voluntarily submit to standardized rules about body shape, clothing and diets.

In western societies, sexual issues appear to be dealt with liberally. Anything can be had on the sexual market, and anything can be discussed. Cuddle parties are offered, in swingers clubs anyone can engage with anyone, and fertilization can be achieved in laboratories.

But none of this has led to the liberation we really desire. In every open heart and in every body there is a burning longing that never finds an anchor, for one door remains locked: The door to the inner animal. Our pure animalistic lustful pleasure remains in its cage. It is never honored by society and continues to prowl along the hidden paths of the unconscious. It makes itself known through illness, sudden fits of rage, depression, and alcoholism – sometimes reaching the surface through an unexpectedly passionate love experience that then ends miserably in the drama of jealousy.

How is a woman in such a threatening world to reveal her true desire? What to do with her secret fantasies in which she is seduced and "taken" by a stranger? Her sexual desires are connected with violence, abuse and perversion and they foment guilt, fear and contempt. She does not want to be violated yet again. The gateway to her true lust can only be opened in a world of trust. But how can trust between the genders, which was shattered so long ago, be restored?

Sexual Revelation, Woman's Shame and Man's Power Game

I am speaking specifically from the point of view of woman, for I would like to tell men something essential about woman; and I would like to encourage women to think and speak about sexuality and bring their desire to light, for that will determine if we manage to create a more beautiful future or not.

Many a woman has experienced revealing herself sexually, in all her lust, to a man, only to be met with his shocked reaction. In the beginning she was self-assured; she loved the game of seduction and enjoyed the thought of being conquered by him. She took pleasure in his advances and began to trust him. Suddenly the boundaries of her shame disappeared. An unusual inner opening made her let go of all her roles and true, deep lust took hold of her. He had awakened a passion in her that she did not yet know. There is a point in sexuality in which a woman has only one desire: Take me fully. It is a vehement point of opening and longing. When a woman is touched in such an intimate, sexual way, then she truly only thinks of one thing, and this is much stronger than the thought of wanting to please the man. She is now pure abandon, to something larger than herself that she cannot give a name to.

Now she needs him. And suddenly she has a deep feeling of total helplessness. Here, she loses her confidence. She only feels deep dependency and neediness. "Don't leave," cries her female soul at this moment. Her self-esteem and her emancipation have disappeared. Now she only seeks and needs a man who can affirm her in her true deep lust and self-revelation. Woman is eternally grateful if in such a moment a man loves and holds her and can respond to her longing. She then feels she has come home. She can be who she truly is. She stands up in bed and starts to dance! Her eyes sparkle with a joy he has never seen in her before. Here, the real love between the sexes begins. But there are not many men on Earth who recognize and therefore love the essence of woman this deeply. A man is usually at a loss when faced with a totally open woman. At first, he is pleased with her full lust, but then he is overpowered. He cannot act as potently as they both would want, and he withdraws. And thus, in the moment of her deepest surrender, she feels abandoned. She feels rejected in her desire, just at the point when she was dependent on him and his acceptance.

She needs to know that his initial withdrawal has nothing to do with rejection or indifference. On the contrary, when he turns away, it is to protect himself from her overpowering sexual presence and her desire. His inner truth is not yet that of the strong man, but that of a son, who adores the Great Mother in the woman, but cannot satisfy her hunger. He longs for her body like someone dying of thirst. He is addicted to her, but he cannot show it without risking her contempt, for he has too often experienced that his neediness repulses a woman. There is hardly a woman who has reached such a level of knowledge and fulfillment that she rests in herself to the point where she can accept the man as he is and be a haven for him. Her own lack of fulfillment makes her see a needy man as an incapable child who is tied to her apron strings. She cannot and does not want to accept him.

Therefore, two unredeemed longings collide. Historically speaking, the man had to find a way out of this drama. He began to pretend to be strong. He began to despise woman for showing her sexual longing, and this contempt gave him a new kind of power and manliness. It was the manliness of the closed heart. It gave him coldness, warrior-like power and sexual potency. He could disguise himself as the strong man that all women fall for. What he couldn't achieve with an open heart, he suddenly achieved through contempt and secret sadism. Films and myths are full of lonely male heroes. The phallus that wouldn't react when faced with the woman who revealed her true nature was replaced by the swords and cannons of the warrior. For many men, it is easier to conquer countries, plan wars and invest in science and research than to understand the essence of a woman. And for women, it often seems easier to submit to the man than to be his partner and reach out to him to discover the land of true potency together. When trying to somehow deal with their own unfulfilled longing, many women also choose to fight and react with contempt. They close off their hearts and punish, with coldness and rejection, the man who dares to show his desire. Woman makes herself unattainable – until a man comes along who can conquer her. She then wants to belong to him fully. But this fight has not helped us either. It has made us forget our true beauty and source. We have forgotten who we really are.

When women overcome their old shame and together come to an understanding, no longer fighting but supporting each other in this point, they gain a new power. The man can then no longer despise her. This gives rise to the possibility of true friendship among women – instead of competition and jealousy. For then they know that they love the same thing about men, and that they do not lose him if he goes to another woman.

A Turning Point in History

Bloodshed on Earth still continues unabated. It is not easy to accept that the reason for the increasing violence, for natural catastrophes, and for the hunger and thirst of people is to be found within us. Dieter Duhm writes that "the environmental crisis is the result of the inner crisis." And at the core of this inner crisis we find constant lovesickness. That is what today determines and suffuses the human world, every office, every parliament and every family. Miraculously though, sensual love never dried up fully. Today, we are at a turning point in history. Everything depends on whether we choose a new direction: towards rediscovered trust, towards the opening of the forbidden gateway.

Although we women have had to go through persecution, the "witches hammer" and many other painful experiences, a part of our soul has remained unharmed. We have not come to this Earth to watch as life is being destroyed, but to care for and protect life. We had to go through a long phase of suffering, fighting and resignation. But the moment we give up the fight, the miracle happens: From deep within, the memory arises of how we are truly meant to be. Every woman who has rediscovered her source is beautiful. She is a sexual being and she can show it again – regardless of whether she has a partner at her side or not. Community arises around such a woman, and she becomes a loving and recognized magnet for people. From this point, we look aghast at the aberrations of the past millennia.

I can only see one way of ending the global tragedy: the trust in love we have lost must be regained. This will create a new field of power for the love between the sexes. The time has come for us to dare to enter the forbidden realm of the senses with our consciousness. A truly divine world wants to be born from deep within, from the mystery of lust. A source of universal love that we have never known wants to be revealed in the moment of total lust and surrender, for in sensual love we are one with our lover, in body, soul, heart and mind. In the magical moment of a sensual embrace we can experience what spiritual seekers, through many years of practice, have been seeking in the mystical union with God. Knowledge, in the deepest sense of the word, and the affirmation of sexual love, no matter what way of life and sexual orientation we choose, are the foundations for a new sensual homecoming on planet Earth. They are the fermenting agent for the new tribes, communities and social structures in which the human being will rediscover home.

Partnership and Free Love

An important preliminary remark to the following chapter: Freedom, trust and truth in love require a corresponding social environment; they need to be embedded in a community of people who trust each other. Only in a community of trust can we experience that one's partner truly does not leave if their erotic interest should lead them to a different person. We need the protective space of a functioning community to really communicate the experiences we have had with another person and make them understandable, where we don't have to immediately react to all the partner's experiences, statements and questions. Experience has shown that if two people try to solve issues that arise in love on their own, they hurt each other needlessly.

We have all surely at least once in our lives been touched by the "high voltage" of life itself that occurs when we fall deeply in love. What a joy! The magical beauty of the whole world reveals itself to us. Nothing is more beautiful than the happiness of two lovers, and hardly anything is more painful than the experience of having love transform into its opposite. We almost all know this process and usually see it as a law of nature.

At first one loves what is different and new in the other person. And since it is so new, we confidently allow ourselves to shower them with all the positive projections at our disposal. She sees the great lover, the prince, or an erotic figure of Christ in the man. In her he sees the essence of womanhood, with her enticing forms and breasts, her seductive and kind smile — both the adored woman and the wild playmate. There are countless poems about approaching her.

In the first weeks, it is as if a magnet draws them together. The fire has been lit. "I love you!" they call out to each other. In loving embraces they discover the unknown in each other. In this unknown a deeply familiar image shines through. It transforms the scents that surround us and our sense of hearing. It is as if one could embrace

Lovers, 2008

the whole world, and one finds the other in everything. It is as if Anima and Animus were celebrating their wedding and a whole universe embraces itself through them. One wants to share everything. The other person's world, both new and familiar, shines into one's own life and casts a spell on everything. There is always something new to discover, and yet one can land in familiar arms. The great dream of a lifelong partnership has been awakened.

Erotically, you desire no one else. You discover each other more and more deeply each time you meet. You discover the secrets and the miracles of the body. It is amazing how deep one can go with each other if mistrust and fear have been replaced by trust. Every gentle touch triggers a surge of energy in the body and results in an ever more encompassing self-revelation. It is the greatest of joys. Neither wants to let go of it; both promise eternal faithfulness.

But this is soon threatened by a gradual fear of abandonment. For have we not known since we were children that whenever we open our hearts, sooner or later we will be punished or rejected? The joy of two lovers will also awaken this memory. And thus, almost imperceptibly, after the first intoxication of love, the question creeps in: "What if I lose this beautiful gift?" Automatically one begins to cling to the other to try to protect the treasure they have found.

They had given their vow of faithfulness in a moment when they were not really able to give it, because they did not know the true depth of it. For a moment our souls are convinced that it will last forever. But soon we are faced with the great challenge of integrating this initial joy into everyday life. Many relationships fail because of it. Without really understanding what is happening, the seventh heaven of love has turned into a tragedy. This, or a similar process played out between millions of lovers, is seen as a personal failure.

We followed a structure that does not correspond to the natural laws of love. Subconsciously, we already know that Eros cannot be tied down. But this only increases our fear of loss. We fight against the obvious until there is no way out. An infinite number of couples find themselves in the same dead end street. There are partners who have been able to maintain a deep friendship, but I know of no monogamous love relationship in which Eros remains permanently alive. The lovers who learn to affirm the freedom of Eros experience its joys often into old age.

In the old tribal cultures, it was normal to stay together for life in full faithfulness and have children together – and at the same time be allowed to experience sexuality with others. Sexuality itself was sacred and not tied to relationships.

It is neither a contradiction nor deceit to long for a partner and at the same time long for erotic adventures. It only becomes deceit if we have to hide it from our partner. Under healthy conditions, it would be a proof of trust if my partner could tell me that he has fallen in love with another woman. Trust would grow if couples could share their intimate experiences with each other. True trust deepens when we can speak our truth. Free love is love without fear. Whether free love succeeds or not depends on our ability to be truthful in love.

The minefield between two lovers is like a prison of traumatic experiences that keeps all of humanity imprisoned in a subtle way. Couples who walk a long path together sooner or later touch this pain. Conflicts are unavoidable. Most people try to solve them in private, but they inevitably get stuck in mutual recrimination. These conflicts cannot be resolved between two people, for the problems they are dealing with are not private mistakes; they are a part of the entire culture and the history of humankind that we all belong to.

Couples who arrive at this point either separate or else agree on living a superficial life together, where they no longer touch their sensitive issues. But they thereby no longer touch their true souls, their core of truth, and the initial love is lost. The explosive material in the minefield consists of repressed wounds from the past. Recollecting them consciously and healing them constitutes deep peace and healing work. Wherever there is consciousness, war cannot happen.

The ability to love is independent of the question of how many relationships I have, whether I am monogamous or polygamous, homosexual or heterosexual, and for some even celibate. These are personal decisions that everyone must make. Here, we do not want to create any new dogmas. The only important thing is under what conditions we arrive at our decisions.

Love is free by its very nature. "Unfree" love is a contradiction in terms; we then mistake something else for love. Perhaps we decide to live monogamously. But we should always remember that one cannot possess another human being. One has no legal claim to love. An environment of free love is not a threat to a monogamous couple. It is only a threat if one does not really trust one's own decision. If both want to live monogamously, it is their free decision. But if one of the two partners suddenly feels differently, then the challenges begin. Am I willing to accept the truth of the other person, or is this the beginning of blackmail? This is a great adventure for two people who have decided to embark on the path of partnership and discover the truth in love.

Some people believe that their drama in love will resolve itself by seeking a new partner whenever problems arise. But the pain and the fear of abandonment in love cannot be overcome by changing partners. Those who run away from love when it becomes difficult will be confronted with their own unresolved issues in every new love relationship. Only those who do not run away from the dark sides of a partnership will go deeper and discover the permanence of love.

An Encounter with Lilith on Malta

Understanding the aspects of the "eternal female" ever more deeply is an essential step on the path towards a culture of partnership. On a journey to Malta I became intimately aware of the figure of Lilith. According to myth, she was Adam's first partner and represents the power of free, untamed Eros. It is difficult to reconcile Lilith with traditional concepts of marriage and faithfulness. I thought of the legends about Lilith, who visits men in their dreams to celebrate the feast of an anonymous encounter. The jealous wives guarded against their husbands being sought out by Lilith, for they suspected that Lilith would awaken in them a longing that would carry them away in the restless desire for other women.

The wives felt that, although now they lived with their longed-for prince in a golden cage, their own longings could not be fulfilled. They had sworn eternal faithfulness in the intoxication of the first joy of love, but now everything had changed. Their longing remained unsatisfied and gave them many restless nights. Every seductive smile from another woman, every plump behind or full breast became a threat to their marriage. Envy and resentment poisoned their originally pure, loving hearts. It also drove away their best girlfriends and they found themselves lonely together with their once-so-desired husbands, who now often seemed distant. The initially thrilling embraces, full of sensual fullness, had become superficial and commonplace. The first signs of frustration and disillusion could be seen in their faces. And so, as the years went by, their initial wildness and beauty turned into the features of frustrated house monsters.

Just as the wife jealously guarded her husband, he also guarded her. Although he perhaps often followed Lilith's tracks – in bars, on business trips or in the shadowy light of brothels – he did this secretly. In the light of day, he was the well-functioning husband who watched over his wife. She was the mother he had bought. He was by a long shot not willing to afford her the adventures he allowed himself. He enjoyed her jealousy, for it gave him the certainty that he could dominate her. They sometimes performed their marital duties, but otherwise their lives had to do with television, money, travel, children, and good food. They filled their lives with inconsequential matters so as not to be reminded of their pain, their unfulfilled love and the great vow that they had once made to each other.

While this was going on, Lilith kept on visiting the bedrooms. Millions and millions of lovers experienced the same fate in love. They thought that their unhappiness was their own personal misery and did not suspect that the same drama was playing out behind all their neighbors' walls. The suppressed Lilith thus controlled the lives of innumerable lovers.

But who is Lilith for us today, after all the centuries of aberrations and confusion? How would she speak to us today? At that morning on Malta she was very close to me and I wrote her words directly into my laptop.

LILITH'S WORDS

I am the wild daughter of the Great Goddess. I am the one who could never be captured. I was Adam's wild bride. I escaped him, even before Eve was supposedly created from Adam's rib and turned into his wife. But I never subordinated myself to man. I was damned by a God whom I had never accepted as such. He could therefore never destroy my wild nature. I am the female primal force in everything that exists. My library is life itself with all its laws of a natural order. I know and recognize the soul of every plant, every animal and every element. Those who do not fear life will also no longer fear my wild nature.

Cultural-historical changes drove the human being out of Paradise. When I saw what had been done to women, I experienced infinite pain and the idea of revenge arose in me. Revenge gave me power, but it also drove me out of my original Paradise and destroyed it.

I have experienced a great history of transformation. Today, I am the historical archetype of the feminine who could initiate the creation of a field of healing of society, for I am connected to the universal processes of healing and a prehistoric culture of peace.

I have never forgotten my roots. But as the Lilith who speaks to you today, I unite the past with a new present. I no longer follow the impulse of revenge, but am paving the way for a new future. In me you will find the germinal force for a new culture of partnership. I have learned to remember and affirm female knowledge. As Lilith I knew separation; I knew pain and disconnection, for I was mistreated and persecuted throughout the centuries. And yet I remained wild and untamable; I could not be imprisoned in the structures of patriarchy. I guarded the pure and elementary Eros that would not let itself be forced into any unnatural forms. I therefore resisted every form of motherliness for a long time, and I even ostensibly defended myself against the Goddess herself. But because I have gone through all this, today I have encompassing knowledge and a comprehensive ex-

The icon "Lust" in the stone circle of Tamera,
designed by Sabine Lichtenfels

perience of female history. I have deeply reconciled myself with the motherly aspects of women. Since I no longer oppose Eve or Mary or any form of motherhood, women have stopped fearing me.

I am now in a greater and deeper connection with healing knowledge, in a new solidarity with everything female. I love the freedom and the adventure of Eros, but I no longer oppose permanence in love. The Madonna and the whore are united within me. Even today, I have never let myself be domesticated, and I have supported women in raising their voices whenever they felt unjustly treated or deceived. I know and accept the personal dream of love – in its clear and unobstructed form – that couples dream, but I always show up whenever I perceive hypocrisy and lies in love. As the wild sister of Eve and Mary, I support women in not letting themselves be belittled or domesticated. We share this work with men so that they again can learn to respect, understand and love us women.

I never succumbed to the seductive offers from men who wanted to buy my love, and I support other women in discovering their own wildness and revealing their true beauty. Every woman becomes beautiful by learning to connect with her own truth again. Whoever follows in my footsteps connects with the voice of a female revolutionary power, and is at the same time taken to the sacred roots of everything female, from where I, too, come. True revolution always means a return to the pure source of evolution. I have led women and men to sexual healing knowledge, for the primary point where peace knowledge has been violated and destroyed lies in the area of sexuality.

My erotic power can only have a healing effect in connection with the whole. This unity contains the healing of jealousy, fear, violence and the pain of loss. Ever since I realized this, something inside me has found peace. Ever since I found the source of my divine nature in Eros, my erotic fullness could have a healing effect. No man or woman can satisfy my desire without this source. I have rediscovered my fulfillment in this source, and it exists within me. My desire therefore no longer burns me up from within. I have learned to listen to the voice of my heart; I know what I need to do and what not.

This process requires a high level of presence. A deep opening was created in my cellular system when I experienced that I can feel totally secure in this world. Since then I can be loving and healing and do not have to hide my wildness and my joy of Eros from anyone. The divine joy of Eros penetrated to the darkest places of the body and is now illuminating it with its light.

I have begun to see how we women can regain our power to produce peace on Earth, in love and in sexuality. Agape – charity – and Eros are no longer opposites. By together studying the laws of Eros ever more deeply, we will understand the logic of the universe ever more deeply. In this way, we can rediscover fulfillment in partnerships, in community and in anonymous encounters.

THE LONGING OF EROS
(LILITHS WORDS, CONTINUED)

The longing of Creation is reflected in the longing of humans. The Earth and the heavens will not rest before this longing is fulfilled.

The longing for the numinous aspect of love, the intense desire that a stranger's glance or simply the form of a body can elicit, as well as the great longing for a couple relationship and partnership, all have the same core: Two beings want to love and know each other in their beauty and freedom. They want to give themselves. They want to reach the deepest depths of communication in elementary physical presence.

It is the primal source of the Goddess that touches us in the fleeting glance of a stranger; it is the longing for the eternal presence of the Goddess, and of being at home with her, that touches us in our longing for permanent intimacy and partnership. It is the memory of the source of Creation from which we all came. It is the memory that, at the deepest level, we are all fully connected in one existence. This is what we wish to rediscover. All our cells want to be permeated by this insight. Nothing alien should separate us any more.

One longing cannot be understood or fulfilled without the other. Neither can find redemption and rest without understanding the aspect of sacredness in sexuality. It is the longing for transformation, for the permanent presence of the divine, that is seeking fulfillment in the longing of the sexes. It is always the Goddess whom the man has seen briefly in the woman and whom he now seeks to encounter – and vice versa.

Fulfillment in love requires being balanced in one's own center and anchoring in inner certainty, with absolute integrity and persistence. Ultimately there is only one answer to all your questions. By holding the thought of wanting to capture and have what one loves for oneself, against the will of the whole, one also begins to kill what one initially loved in the other. No Goddess will ever let herself be conquered and no freedom will ever let itself be locked up in a cage. The issue of love will only find its solution through connection with the whole. In this connection we find the healing of jealousy, fear, and violence, as well as of the pain and fear of being abandoned. This is how we can find fulfillment in our partnerships, fulfillment in community and fulfillment in anonymous encounters. You will discover that they all belong together and cannot be lived separately from each other.

I am Soul, I am Flesh

Will religions still exist in a new culture? One thing is sure: The elementary powers of Eros and sexuality will no longer be suppressed in the temples, cathedrals and altars of the future. Instead, the sacredness of Eros will be at the center of a humane culture and it will be celebrated and honored. Let us again listen to the words of the eternal feminine:

Eros and religion are the two fundamental forces that must come together for healing to occur. For I not only have a soul – I am soul. I am a soul who wishes to provide a home for the divine power. In the Kabbalah I am called Shekhina – the soul or the house of God.

As a soul I have made my home in the body. This is what is meant by: "The word became flesh." It is in the tension between Logos and Eros – between word and matter – that a decision is made determining whether humanity will rise up again or perish.

The sexual world and the divine world want to show themselves in me as one single world. This miracle wants to be rediscovered and seen in all things earthly, physical and human. The secret of Sexus lies in my flesh. In the moment when man sees this in me, when he can understand my soul physically, I begin to shine brightly. In these moments, both bodies are permeated by the miracle of sexual love. And they knew each other: In this moment I have come home!

But if the spiritual regions of the soul and the sexual regions of the flesh are in conflict for too long, impatience and latent rage arise in me. This is the great disaster of the masculine religions: They have abducted the soul from the Earth and from all life.

But I am awakened by the conscious touch of my carnal aspect. There, the entire miracle of the divine world is revealed. Here, we also find the true secret of permanence in love. Here, everything female regains its initial power. What we called God becomes a celebration of life. The entire Earth is a secret of sensual love that is revealing itself. This is not about direct sex – that too – but about the right way to deal with the soul in all material life.

As a woman, for man I am the revelation of ensouled flesh. To reveal myself, I need the "knowing" man. When you, man, recognize me, you are also my midwife – just as I can help you recognize yourself as my lover through my body.

In me, Adam discovers Lilith and Eve together in one body. He discovers her as if for the first time, and she feels seen and recognized by him. This is where the decision is made on whether we will have war or peace. It is from this source that life springs anew.

To all Son-Men

First, a preliminary note: Every man's love of a woman is determined by his love for his mother. In every beloved woman, no matter how old, he always sees the archetype of the mother. In the love school at Tamera we keep hearing deep stories about the love between mother and son. This is how one man summarized his insights:

"The contact with my mother was the first source of love in my life. This intimate contact broke off the moment an erotic longing arose. She could not give me the erotic appreciation that I, as an adolescent, would have needed; morals and fear were too strong. Of course, this happens not only to me, but to all men. For a man this loss is extremely painful, for as he loses his intimate relationship with his mother, he also loses the feeling of home, security and acceptance. Many male philosophies are protective mechanisms designed to block this pain. But the longing remains; he seeks his opposite in every woman, and he seeks erotic recognition – and under no circumstance does he want to feel the pain of separation again. The only way men have learned to deal with this is through the oppression of women. This is how patriarchy is reestablished, again and again. Patriarchy is a system of anger, especially the anger of the son-men, whose love of their mothers and of the feminine could not be lived. Anger is love energy that is searching for a channel to express itself. I feel an inner ocean of tears every time I see a young soldier whose anger has been instrumentalized for war. He could, without a doubt, be me! At some point I understood that my mother was once a daughter and had touched her own points of pain. My compassion with the fate of women was also healing for me."

In the previous chapters, I described Lilith as the wild, erotic aspect of the eternal feminine. Her counterpart is Maria, the power of compassion, of benevolent love, the archetype of the mother. What would Maria say to men today, at the end of patriarchy? What words does she find for the pain and the lovesickness that men keep repressing and compensating for by abusing power and being violent?

One early morning I put myself in the position of this archetype and wrote down her words to men:

The pain that accumulates in your soul is the pain of all men who never truly found a home with their mothers. All loving sons have experienced this pain. Your soul's greatest yearning is to be both the lover and the liberator of your mother. It was the heavenly sweetness of your mother that made you come to this planet in the first place. But you soon felt that a part of her was not present; she was enveloped in a quiet sadness. She was always gone. But hidden behind a thousand veils, she still always reminded you of an unredeemed promise that called out for fulfillment. From early on, this made your soul drunk with longing and desire.

Your mother was the slave of a husband and had to hide her loving heart from the jealous eyes of her lord. Not only her husband, but all of society was her lord, her tyrant, and the yoke under which her loving soul was bent. The sensual fairy whom you had worshiped had transformed into a hissing mother animal, who lured and threatened you, demanded you be strong and early on controlled you through her own frustration.

At the same time, you were the goal of her longing, her secret lover, her knight, her prince. You were supposed to liberate her from the claws of a husband who could not fulfill what she longed for. In her frustrated arrogance towards him, you felt the contempt of the entire female gender against men. The young and childish soul within you also sensed that the father had failed, and therefore so had the entire male gender. Through her eyes you sensed her saying: "Perhaps you are able to do what your father could not: Take me back to my true beauty as a loving being, in my wildness and playfulness. Perhaps you will be able to bring my primal feminine song to life, to let my heart feel and my body pulsate by liberating the lover in me that I truly am."

The secret and hopeless love between mother and son has laid itself like an iron ring around your heart. This iron ring surrounds millions of men's hearts and has turned them into cold warriors, soldiers and heroes, researchers, businessmen and office workers, instead of lovers and caretakers of all creatures.

Know that still today it is the projection on the mother that separates you from your beloved. It is the mother you are fleeing from when you flee from your beloved. It is for the lost mother that you shed your tears when you believe that you are losing your beloved. It is the mother you want to hold on to when the jealous lover awakens in you; he is fighting against the overpowering father.

The pain you feel is a historical pain. All sons have at some point experienced it, because the soul of the mother and of the loving woman were banished from your culture. You and your loving heart wanted to worship her and her sensual beauty – but an entire society humiliated and demonized her. All her sensuality, everything sexual, was considered impure and disgraceful. The beautiful image of your mother transformed in front of your eyes into something devilish and demonic. Because she was damned for her sexual nature, she had to banish everything that reminded her of it – including her son. When you wanted to test your male awakening at her breasts, she rejected you, for she could not tolerate and respond to your erotic joy. This rejection kept deepening the chasm between love and lust within you and within all son-men.

At the same time, her desire is overpowering. The young son senses the secret and forbidden pact with his mother that nobody must know about, and he suffers under its burden. She bound herself to you through her unfulfilled yearning – the eternal bond of a secret love that was never fulfilled. You began to mimic the adult, the lover, the virile man that you were nowhere close to being, only to pass the test in her eyes.

In the beginning you wanted your father to be your friend and companion. But he long ago became your competitor. To win the mother, one would have to conquer the father. You did not know that your father originally was an unfulfilled son-man too, who had to take possession of his mother, because he did not feel he could fulfill her sensual yearning. He thus transformed into the possessive father archetype. Legions of sons have rebelled against their fathers, and yet ultimately turned into copies of them. Legions of fathers had to step down from their thrones, and were ultimately exposed as unredeemed sons.

And still today every mother waits for the man who sees and supports her womanhood, also sexually. The archetype of the sensual lover is still waiting to be born. There is no other way out: If you want healing, you must leave the system of love that you came from. See to it that a new way is found. Transform your rage into a desire for the insights that are needed to conquer and transform this dragon of an entire culture. Rediscover your original trust through love of the feminine essence, of the body, of nature, of the world and its sensual beauty – we can call it the power of the Goddess.

The Goddess is not a religion; she is life itself. You can find her in every woman. Your trust in her transforms your relationship with all women. If you wish to understand the world, first become a witness to how she works. Let go of the arrogance that was supposed to protect you from love, and again accept that all life has a soul. Those who have accessed the sacred source of life are compassionate. They experience the hunger and the joy, the suffering and the happiness of all beings. They take the responsibility of a gentle lover and midwife for all things that are awakening.

When women and men have seen through and overcome their power struggles; when they no longer wait for each other and yet see to what extent they are a part of the whole that needs them; when they realize that they can find their joint anchor in a higher world and in a higher self, then they are approaching an insight that is waiting to be born: And they knew each other – a man and a woman – and a wonderful path of sensual love can begin, a path of love that is no longer bound to any conditions.

CHAPTER 2:
KEY PERSONAL EXPERIENCES

WHERE HAVE ALL THE FATHERS GONE?

Where have all the young men gone?
Long time passing
...Gone for soldiers everyone
Oh, when will they ever learn?

~Lyrics by Pete Seeger

Much has been written about son-men and the relationship between mother and son. But how about the daughters' relationship with their fathers?

Here, I could almost write the same thing as I wrote in the introduction to my address to the son-men. For us women, too, the mother is the first source of love. Here, much is determined about our trust in life and in the world and about our womanhood. We subconsciously take on almost all the issues that our mothers have not resolved, and we repeat their patterns of behavior. But very soon our father gains an enormous importance for our lives. Every girl once loved her father, no matter how much he may have been a tyrant. One can almost not fathom what goes on in the soul of a young woman when she suddenly has to realize that her father was co-responsible for a cruel and fascist system. Some women need an entire lifetime to deal with such unresolved tensions in her soul.

For most women of my generation, the contact with the father was characterized by his absence and excessive strictness. Mother was there for the children, for the immediate surroundings, for the intimate care, whereas father was responsible for the world. Closer things were often annoying to him. My father studied his musical scores, read books, played the piano – and we children were supposed to be quiet whenever he was in the house. This always surrounded him with an aura of a certain authority. I was only allowed to play with Daddy during the holidays or sometimes on Sundays.

I, personally, was lucky, for my father represented a certain male kindness and a compassion for the fate of the world. I loved him above everything else and I was always sure that he loved me. Often, when playing outside, I had the feeling that Daddy was watching me lovingly. He sees everything and he knows everything. I wanted to know as much, be able to do as many things and be as recognized as he was.

Having my mother as a role model was more difficult. As children we had the feeling that she had to put us and father above all her own longings. That was normal; not only in our family, but for all my girlfriends.

As a small child I was sometimes allowed to sit in Daddy's lap and have my arms around his neck. But when I grew older there was a break in this, too. Increasingly, the contact had to occur on the mental-spiritual plane. I can well remember how I once proudly did cartwheels in front of Daddy and some uncles and aunts. I was perhaps seven years old and only had transparent panties on. Daddy warned me that he did not want me to show myself that way in front of adults – I was too old for that. This was the first time that shame consciously entered into my life.

The intimate contact broke off entirely when my erotic awakening occurred. During puberty he increasingly turned into the strict, punishing father who watched jealously over the life of his daughter. I can well remember that I asked myself if he even knew anything about me.

We were able to talk about music, about world events and harmonic research – those were wonderful conversations – but we could not talk about love. And when I told him I wanted to realize some of the things we had talked about, he admonished me sternly: "See to it that you graduate first."

My childish soul thus realized early on that if I showed the world what I really love, I would be punished. He will only love me as long as I follow his instructions. Many basic beliefs crept in that I, still today, notice in my relationship with men.

I yearned for an approving word about the first signs of my growing breasts. I would have loved having a father whom I could have asked all the questions I had about my first infatuations. But there was an absolute taboo against erotic topics.

And yet, as a pubescent teenager I carried a photo of my father in my purse. My first boyfriend was supposed to be like him, as wise, intelligent, artistic, loving and thoughtful as he. This gave rise to a double bind: his strong love of me that I sensed – and the lack of sensual appreciation at close range.

Most women have had similar experiences. The lack of fathers at close range gives rise to a corresponding lack of self-confidence in becoming a woman. We were warned against strangers; they accosted us everywhere and showed their sexual reaction openly, often in an inconsiderate way. But nobody had introduced us to the erotic world so that we could have shown, without fear, what we loved and what we did not. There was thus an attraction to the forbidden world of Eros, but it was drenched in fear. The only way we could deal with it was to find a friend, a man, who would provide the protection and intimacy that we so longed for and that we had sought in vain in our fathers. He would put his protective arms around us and abduct us to the paradise we longed for.

As time went by, we discovered that the fulfillment of the promise of love that we longed for did not exist anywhere on Earth. The result was rage against our fathers and against a world that we felt was fraudulent, rage against sexual harassment by men and their constant attempts to patronize and control us. There were only two ways out: Rage and emancipation – or submission. It wasn't until later that I understood that my father, too, had once been a son who yearned for his mother, and that already when I was a young girl,

Heike, scratching her feet, 2004

he saw his mother in me. He had once loved her very much, but approaching her in a sensual way was an absolute taboo. I never fully abandoned my love of my father, but I became a rebel. I challenged him whenever I could. Whenever he forbade something, I defied him. "Now, more than ever!"

My rage came from love. I wanted to show him that I, too, am someone. I identified with the rebellious Antigone, who demanded that her father acknowledge her – the way she wanted to be, not the way he wanted her to be. But behind all the rebellion there was still the great love of my father.

As a young woman, I didn't make things easy for men. My friend and I excited and challenged men with all the charm we had as teenagers. We did not know, at that time, what we triggered in them. We knew very little about what goes on sexually under the surface, but then, how could we have? It was the allure of the unknown and of what was forbidden that attracted us. At night I secretly climbed out the window when my parents were asleep and went to bars to learn more about this forbidden world of Eros. Even today, I am thankful for my guardian angel, for I ventured into dangerous zones. I believe that not many mature men today are aware of the importance they hold for young women.

For a young woman it is in no way always about sex; it is just as much about the missing sensual recognition by the father. As a 16-year-old I lay down in the bed of a 32-year-old man, simply because I wanted to be close to him sensually. I wanted to try things out without being exploited by him. He was sensitive enough to not abuse me. But what man can deal adequately with this high voltage female yearning? When she throws herself into his arms with all her female charm, what man can then guide, hold and lovingly support her, instead of being at the mercy of his own unfulfilled desires?

Only few young women know that behind the façade of the mature man there is often an insecure man who is pretending to be strong, but is usually full of unfulfilled sexual desires that he cannot share with anyone. We know how much misery in love comes from mis-directed projections. Behind every macho man, there is a wounded son who could never get close to his mother – and who later, as an adult, was equipped with instruments of power by society. But he is seldom the lord of his house, for it is usually his unsatisfied longings that control him. He tries to hide his inner drives for as long as he can and hides behind the façade of decency until they finally break through. The same tragedy always plays out in the fight between the sexes: We are seeking something in the other that cannot be found there. It is only by becoming conscious of this background, and by establishing new social systems in which these issues can be seen under the protection of a community, that we can resolve this drama.

MY EXPERIENCE WITH MY TEACHER OF RELIGION

My girlfriend and I both fell in love with our religious studies teacher. We flirted with him whenever we could. Finally, after many years, the time had come. During one of our class excursions, in a barn, the three of us had a wonderful sensual experience, a loving erotic game with kisses and embraces. The next morning, I was blissful and had a thousand butterflies in my stomach. We were in the grips of high sensual magic. From my point of view, it was not a teacher using or seducing his students. Instead, it was three people, following the sensual joy they took in each other. We definitely wanted it – we seduced him, even if we at the time did not really know what we were doing.

In my joy and naïveté, I wanted to go to his wife the next day and tell her of our joy, for I also liked and admired her and felt close to her through my experience with her husband. But then came the cosmic hammer from a social structure in which something that was so beautiful could not be allowed. When I asked him how we should tell his wife about it, he said, "She won't understand," and asked that we tell nobody about it. It was as if my young soul had been stabbed with a knife. We had just felt so free and suddenly we were prisoners in a web of dishonesty, in a world of false morals and phony decency. What was originally pure and beautiful was transformed through our distress and guilt into something diabolical. I was initiated into a system in which women automatically become competitors. I suddenly saw myself as a traitor: cheating on a woman whom I admired. This did not at all correspond to my inner truth. It was difficult for us to not have anyone with whom to share our joy and our confusion.

From my point of view, his real guilt was not that he had played along in an erotic game with us, but that he had introduced us to the system of lies and secrecy. Thus started the aberration in love – a net of lies, in which so many get ensnared. I understand women who in such a situation direct their disappointment at men; I understand their raging anger and despair.

At the time I was mature enough not to blame him personally. What should he have done? His profession and his marriage were at stake. Instead, I began to see through the disgrace of a social system that for centuries has been built on lies in the area of love. Even today I am thankful that he then told me: "In love, you will do it all differently." And he turned out to be right. I accepted his wish to keep our erotic encounter secret from his wife, for he was an authority for us, but when I was adult enough, I told him that this had been a deep mistake. And I was right: As he read in his wife's diary after she died, his wife had guessed it all back then. This was a reason for me to distance myself from a system of love that makes lying necessary.

A Rape Prevented

I would like to describe a different example that strengthened my decision to commit myself to creating a new system in love. In my life I have had several experiences in which I narrowly avoided being raped. Each time, faced with a dangerous situation that was seemingly hopeless, I experienced something different: the presence of a helping power.

I experienced one such situation at the age of 17. I was on my way home late at night. Every day I had to walk part of the way from the bus stop through a forest. A stranger, who must have been observing me, had hidden behind a tree. Suddenly, he jumped out and grabbed me. Immediately, my inner guidance set in and looked for a way out. It seemed to know exactly what I had to do to avert the danger. If I were to scream, it would only have increased his lust. To wrench myself free was also not an option, for he was much too strong. Without thinking, I said with a calm, deep voice: "Please don't; I'm very sick. I have salmonella." His erotic excitement was gone immediately. The strong sexual tension that was based on him being the perpetrator and I a helpless victim, was gone, and he let go of me. "Salmonella, what's that?" he stuttered. I remained standing, and suddenly I even felt compassion for him and told him that he needed to find other ways to approach a woman.

When we had said goodbye, my knees were shaking. Only then did I understand what had just happened. Today, I know I must have had a lot of luck or a guardian angel that others do not have in similar situations. Violence is often so overpowering and is instrumentalized in such a way that an individual can find no way out. I know many women who have been abused and became victims of cruel violent crimes.

My question is: Can we learn to extend the protective force that I experienced there to all women? Can we create a society in which there is basic knowledge about sexuality that helps prevent every kind of violent crime? I am sure that if we understand the reasons for sexual crime, we will step by step learn to create conditions in which there are no more sex offenders and no more victims.

Babette (Sabine), 2001

A PROJECT TO "SAVE LOVE"

In 1978 I met Dieter Duhm, who had been a spokesperson for the students' movement and had become quite well-known through his book *Fear in Capitalism* (Angst im Kapitalismus). He had been traveling throughout Germany and other countries for several years to contact interesting researchers and projects. Together with my long-time friend Rainer Ehrenpreis, we decided to establish the so-called "Bauhütte"[3] – a peace research community and holistic university to bring together areas of knowledge that in normal universities were separated from each other, or were not taught at all. Our idea was to establish a nonviolent cultural model in which holistic peace knowledge would be developed for a new culture. The early group rented a small farm in Southern Germany. Soon, people who were interested came from the most varied directions – from the political left, spiritual groups, art, science and welfare organizations. In spite of the initial enthusiasm, it soon became clear that the establishment of the research areas would not go smoothly. We experienced the typical conflicts that arise in the establishment of every group. We realized that we had to find a new way of dealing with and solving interpersonal conflicts, and that developing knowledge about creating communities and especially about love, partnership and sexuality would constitute core areas of research for a new culture.

We learned to no longer keep budding infatuations secret from each other, but made them the object of our research. We wanted to find out under what social conditions love and faithfulness, truth and freedom are possible. A main research question was: "How can we live together so that the sexual attention from one person to another does not give rise to so much fear, anger and jealousy in a third person?" We struggled for many years to combine the great longing for

---

[3] In the middle ages, a "Bauhütte" or "builder's hut" was a hut or lodge erected at the site where a gothic cathedral was to be built to prepare the different steps in its construction.

intimate love between two people with a life in freedom, especially in sexual freedom.

We were thereby confronted with many prejudices and moral beliefs in society – in the public realm, in our neighborhood, in our parental homes and in ourselves as well. We realized that we had to deal with and resolve subconscious fears and taboos in ourselves to find a more encompassing love and faithfulness. We realized how much power this underground of suppressed emotions, fears and moral attitudes has in society and how much power we still allowed it to have in our lives when we gave way to blind attacks of jealousy, possessiveness or even romantic ideas about love. To shine the light of consciousness into these areas was a voyage of discovery without end.

Nothing human was strange to us. With tears and laughter, we revealed our secret loves, erotic confessions and sexual fantasies. We were surprised to find that almost everybody had similar fantasies. We spent hours and days together, spoke about issues that are normally never discussed, and about hopes and fears. We put our most hidden thoughts on the stage with the help of art and theater and we learned to become visible to each other and recognize who we truly are. We discovered the value of trust in a community. Protected by it, the partners in a love relationship could say things to each other that they couldn't have said otherwise. Slowly but surely, we approached the areas of the soul where true love becomes possible.

We had made the great discovery that what is most secret and intimate is not private. One's entire life, and every human society, is permeated by secret thoughts and the suppression of sexual desires. They form a substrate in society that makes honest exchange and cooperation within a group extremely difficult, causing every utopia to fail. This substrate dissolves in a community in which it is possible to communicate truthfully, also about emotional abysses and secret fantasies. We understood deeply that it is only in the spirit of compassion that the mighty hidden sexual force can manifest without creating chaos. It is only in the spirit of compassion that the eternal dream of true partnership between man and woman will become reality.

We were courageous in public as well; sometimes, in our youthful folly, perhaps a bit too courageous. Our statements were provocative and taken as a threat by some – but this was not at all our intent. This ultimately caused enmities to arise. In the 1980s there was a media campaign throughout Germany and Switzerland with headlines such as "Sex Clinic in the Black Forest" or "Orgy with 150 couples." There were no limits to the fantasies expressed in these articles. What was most painful was the grotesque statement that we promoted sex with children. Nothing was further from the truth. On the contrary, one of our deepest motives was to embed sexuality among adults within trust and truth, specifically so that children would be protected against the abuse of sexually pent-up adults.

Among other things, we were said to be a subsidiary organization of the AAO (Aktionsanalytische Organisation [Action Analytical Organization]) in Austria. In 1999 its founder, Otto Mühl, was sentenced to seven years in prison for child abuse and the community was dissolved. In search of a social alternative, Dieter Duhm had visited the commune several times in its early years, once even for several months. The last time he was there was in 1979. In the beginning he was inspired and enthusiastic about the commune; but then, for various reasons, he distanced himself from it. Only very few of us ever visited the place. And yet it kept on being publicly repeated that we were a subsidiary organization. For a while this intensified the suspicion of child abuse.

For us it was a time of testing and awakening. We experienced first-hand what it meant to be a fringe group in society, a black sheep. We saw how the same process called forth enmity everywhere: Those who feel threatened and attacked automatically go on the attack so as not to be hurt. This reaction happens so fast that it usually occurs subconsciously. The result hit us harder than I could have imagined possible in a democratic country. The not-for-profit status of our association was revoked. The owners of the property where we were living imposed stricter conditions. Construction applications were revoked. When Dieter Duhm wanted to speak in public, the organizers were warned against us and often canceled the events at short notice. Bookshops took our books from their shelves. Those who took our side were soon also branded a "cult." It was like a public gag order. And yet all these attacks could not destroy us, for we had learned to look all our mistakes in the eye and were no longer afraid of the denunciations of others. Our inner cohesion gave us the strength to persevere.

Today the community has become so stable that it can no longer break apart due to interpersonal conflicts – and it is therefore also strongly protected against attacks from outside. Our forty years of experience in establishing community has given rise to a field of solidarity and creativity that other recently founded communities can now profit from.

Time and again we are asked: "How did you make it?" It was by doing what many people had warned us against: We took on the topic of Eros and remained faithful to it through all the conflicts. In spite of being branded a cult and other slander, we never kept silent about the issue, and that gave our work a clear direction.

The establishment of our project required us to go through a challenging process. We had to learn not to react to attacks with fear, anger or enmity. Our intent to establish a holistic peace project thus first had to be fulfilled from within. We could train ourselves to overcome fear, rage and violence. This provided a solid basis for our work.

Today, our basic knowledge about sexuality also helps us in our political work in crisis areas. We are able to create spaces of truth, for example, for women who have been raped and never spoken about it or for men who do not know what to do with their dammed-up sexuality.

At the same time, I do not see us as having reached the goal of combining the very intimate quality of partnership with free, knowing sexuality. We need a social framework in which truth and trust among people is possible and in which the youth can find orientation. Only then will sexual violence truly end.

Sometimes we felt like salmon in the water, which always swim against the current. This is how we made things possible that others regarded as being impossible.

FAITHFULNESS AND FREEDOM BELONG TOGETHER

There is a longing for erotic adventure and a longing for personal love and partnership experienced and practiced daily. Hardly anyone dares to pursue both these longings. The attempts to combine them have resulted in too much pain. Most people today require that their partners choose: either the path of partnership or the path of remaining single with occasional sexual adventures. In monogamous partnerships the door to others is usually firmly closed and eternal faithfulness is sworn to each other – and then, since time immemorial, they break their vow.

When I got to know my partner, I thought I had already overcome jealousy. But when we became increasingly intimate with each other, I had to go through it all over again and learn what truly dissolves it. My beloved was a man with a large heart for women. Almost every woman falls in love with such a man. After he had spent almost every night with me, I had to admit that a fear of being abandoned slowly crept in. Our sexuality had entered into areas that neither of us had experienced before. We were now very intimate with each other, and I did not want to lose it. I suddenly started paying attention to what he would do next. I had become emotionally dependent. Suddenly I came to a point where my soul cried out: "Don't leave me!"

At the time I was not able to formulate this clearly. I was ashamed of my neediness and tried to hide it as long as I could. I have observed this process in many women. When they are ready to give themselves entirely to a man, they suddenly question their own attractivity, and this is the moment when other women become threats to them. I noticed in myself an additional, typically feminine process: When we love a man, we tend to lose our own source. We are then only focused on HIM. And because we have lost ourselves, jealousy and rage ensue.

I had a key experience at a time when my partner and I shared especially deep sexual experiences with each other. We had discovered language during sex. We could communicate things without it interrupting the sexual process; on the contrary, it heightened it. The sexual encounter became a process of deepest self-revelation. For me, these experiences were absolutely complete and fulfilling. They made my soul feel full. Here, it became true: A man and a woman knew each other. Afterwards, I could lie there for hours, nestling his body and only listening to my inner emotional and bodily processes. In such moments, I could have said, "I now feel monogamous." I felt no desire for any other adventures.

For him, it seemed to be totally different. He was so deeply charged by our sexual experiences and his erotic power was burning so strongly that he could have passed it on to many others. The erotic love of the essence of woman had awakened fully in him. But what woman who is in love can understand this anarchic, wild side of a man? The terror of anonymous Eros thus suddenly clouded our happiness. The woman at the cash register in the supermarket, the neighbor in the house across the street – everywhere he was tempted by promises of erotic joy. I was jealous. I thought there was something he couldn't find in me and therefore wanted to go to others. It was only after he had related a dream he had that I understood the male side more deeply. It was not that something was missing for him; on the contrary: It was his happiness with me that inspired him to also go in other directions.

He had dreamt of an unknown, beautiful woman, as enticing as Lilith in her sexual temptation, who stood on a balcony and waved for him to come to her. I stood next to her, smiled and welcomed both him and her. He could and was allowed to simply follow this invitation. This dream healed something in my soul. I now felt that he was not running away from me when he desired another woman. Instead, something wanted to connect. Triggered by this dream, the intimate wanted to connect with the unknown and Mary wanted to unite with Lilith, within me. Mary, the archetype of the mother and the companion could share in the sexual joy between the two. I experienced directly how much a man loves the mother in every lover who can affirm his opening to others instead of punishing him for it. My jealousy disappeared through this dream image alone. Something calmed down deep within me. I understood men better in their search and their desire. I also understood the essence of Eros better: We remain connected to Eros if we do not feel excluded and do not compare ourselves with others. If we succeed in this, something shifts in the relationship between the genders. The latent war dissolves, as does the feeling of separation, for he never really left. We are still together today.

Thanks to this process, I was able to unite two archetypes within myself that would otherwise always remain separate: that of the wild Lilith and of Mary, the intimate companion. Mary is a motherly, benevolent force. Normally, a woman is appalled when the man discovers the mother in her: She compares herself to the wild, erotic Lilith and now feels less desired, bored, excluded from Eros. But that is a mistake. By uniting the two sides in me, I could truly become his partner in solidarity and our sexual bliss deepened. For me this reconciliation with the female archetypes within a woman is an important key for giving Eros permanence in a relationship, keeping it from being destroyed by comparisons and jealousy.

It is an erotic truth that the loving embrace and the trust we experience with a partner can awaken the longing to share it with others, too. This is not a threat to a relationship; instead, it is a wonderful secret. Something new is awakened in a partnership when we discover that we are allowed to love others too, including sexually. We discover that Eros becomes permanent, specifically by setting it free. The more I include of the world in my embraces, the more alive and expansive our erotic experience becomes.

And by the way, through the years I learned not to be ashamed of the neediness that occasionally arose, but to let him know when I needed his presence, without claiming it as a right.

Kostas – a Sexual Experience on the Island of Corfu

I would like to relate a very special moment in my life when I had an experience of free love that delighted me in my deepest core. At this moment I felt: "Oh, that is how it's meant to be! That's how life wants to be lived." I already lived in a solid partnership, I was a mother and a beloved, about 30 years old. In the middle of this world, anonymous Eros struck like lightning into my life. I experienced the deep joy that occurs when the free flow of Eros is allowed and does not create a contradiction to an intimate love relationship.

We had traveled to Greece in a small group. We sat at a café in front of a butcher's shop. That's when it happened! It was the butcher's gaze that went right through me. I was sitting in a group of friends, my children and my partner, but in my soul I was elsewhere. And I knew – there HE is. What should I do now?

Normally, we do not even speak about such events. If we were to follow our desire, we would immediately go over and say: "Come with me." But shame and the fear of rejection and contempt paralyze us, as do the rules of social decency. So, what to do?

My partner knows me very well and immediately noticed that something was happening inside me. I then told my friends right away and straightforwardly what was going on in my soul. What a gift it is for a woman to be able to tell her partner such things without him becoming enraged! An entire soul pattern shifts if in such a moment a woman is not punished or subjected to fits of rage or has to fear him leaving her, but instead immediately receives his empathy. If in this moment the man does not demand love from me or make claims on me, but reacts with interest, is this not a key to true partnership? Would we not deeply love any partner who also retains these qualities in challenging situations?

My girlfriend, who sat at our table, said immediately: "Go ahead, invite him!" It took me two hours to get up my courage to take this step. I trembled with excitement, and then I took the leap. I stepped into his shop and, standing blushing at the counter, said: "I know that you want to meet me. We don't have to talk very much. We don't first have to have a drink somewhere or go to a disco. I simply want to meet you sexually."

He answered: "Of course I'd like to meet you. But you are here with your partner, with your family. It is impossible."

"No, my partner knows about it. It is possible."

He looked at me in surprise and gave me a card from a place where we could meet. We arranged a time and I went back to my table, relieved.

We met. We didn't even know each other's name, but we had a sexual encounter of the kind that you never forget for the rest of your life. We followed our sensual lust without holding back. Our chemistry was right at all levels and I did not have to do anything extra to please him. Nor did he experience any performance pressure. Instead, we let our love game unfold like natural animals and followed our deep lust.

Afterwards, I asked him to come with me to meet my partner. He looked at me incredulously, but followed me to our apartment nearby. This was a very special moment in my life when, somewhere in Greece, these two men met each other. After a moment of uncertainty, my partner offered him a glass of whisky. They raised a toast – to me, this "wonderful woman" – and my partner began to tell him what he loved about me. Then Kostas began to truthfully describe what fascinated him so much about me and our encounter. Again and again they laughingly clinked their glasses and became increasingly creative in their hymns of praise to the eternal female. I can hardly describe what I felt: "This is how life is meant to be," were the few words I managed to say. It was as if the burdens of centuries were lifted from me – centuries of fear of punishment and persecution can dissolve if we reveal our true sensual nature.

I am telling this story because it touches the place where fear can turn into trust. A new archetypal image of love between a man and a woman found its fulfillment here. I loved my beloved endlessly for his openness. A man will not lose his beloved so easily to another if he retains his openness and interest in her, even in moments when she turns to another man. If a man affirms this adventurous side of his beloved, their joint Eros increases. Let us build a world in which this truth between partners becomes possible. Not fear, but trust, is the elixir that makes permanent love between two people possible.

True partnership is never built exclusively on Eros. If I am able to be at the forefront of truth, without demanding love, then Eros does not decrease; it increases.

My Experience During Forty Years of Partnership

After almost forty years of partnership, I can say from experience that our erotic adventures have enriched our love lives enormously. Our trust has not decreased, but increased, and Eros never dried up. We discovered that the faithfulness that we long for so much was enriched specifically by allowing the unknown into our love relationship.

I was able to heal my fear of being abandoned in love by deciding to no longer abandon what I love. Love by its nature leads to permanence. What I truly love, I cannot abandon. But if I run away from the depths that love demands of us, the erotic adventures will also in time become stale. In this sense, one can say that partnership and free love do not exclude each other; they complement each other.

Eventually, we will realize that partnership is a cultural asset. We cannot develop partnerships in our current culture, for it contradicts the essence of partnership. A relationship based on partnership means not putting anyone above or below ourselves, not patronizing or controlling anyone or being patronized or controlled by anyone. Instead, we will always ask who our partner truly is, what he or she wants and needs, and what his or her soul is seeking and loves. Once we have learned to be in partnership with everything around us, this knowledge will lead us to our personal partnerships, if that is what is wanted. Our feeling of self-worth will no longer depend on if we have a love partner or not.

Nobody can build a partnership based only on the foundation of Eros. Permanent love relationships arise by taking joint responsibility and empathizing and caring for the world. They also arise by supporting each other in difficult situations and overcoming them together. Our partnership has remained alive and vibrant until today because of our common interest in the healing of this planet. We have joint projects, goals and issues. That is what keeps bringing us together. Whenever jealousy and the fear of being abandoned are replaced by a genuine interest in each other, love and faithfulness are strengthened in a way that no wedding ring can achieve.

B. mit Buch
von Dorothee Mclean
am Strand von
Zambujeira
16/4/2007
15

Babette (Sabine) with a book by Dorothy Maclean
at the beach of Zambujeira, 2007

At the Source of the Feminine

Sometimes, during a morning walk or when smelling the scent of apple blossoms, a primal memory awakens in me. It is the sense of a large presence, the reality of a force of peace that wants to enter our material life – a power that seduces me through smells, light, sound and abundance. It is a paradise that has a thoroughly earthly quality: I can feel, see, smell, hear and taste it. My body becomes a temple of wonderful awareness. Now I have arrived – within myself and in the world.

Around me church bells are ringing and in it I hear a goodbye. It is the goodbye from an era that was characterized by imperialist religions and institutions. In it we were homeless, constantly seeking – and since we ourselves were refugees, we drove away others. But now I am surrounded by a wonderful light that is more present, more powerful and more real than everything that humanity has realized on this planet during the past millennia.

I am shocked to realize that I – a woman – never really felt at home within myself. I never loved myself and always had the feeling that I had to be different than I am. Even when I was acknowledged for my achievements or my beauty, I could not accept it. Something in me was always "too:" too fat, too thin, too big, too small, too fast, too slow. Something was always making comparisons and was never ok. How would I ever be able to love a man, if I did not love myself?

But now – flooded by a memory – I recognize that I am of a divine nature – I am complete. I have arrived in the reality of a shining universe, in something we call Eternity. I have experienced myself as the one I am and the one I will be.

This is where my real revolution begins. It is no longer a fight against an old world. It is the return to the powers of evolution, which carry all the knowledge for the emergence of a new culture. This is where the liberation from the claws of a traumatic history begins.

Peace begins with the acceptance and affirmation of all living beings. By learning to affirm the present, I receive the power to see our mistakes and imperfections, learn from them and build a new culture.

Now that I have found my anchor in presence again, I no longer have to flee from this world. I no longer am afraid of the dichotomies of life, because I know that everything that is sacred is anchored in eternity. I see the goal of humanity in front of me and I love it. I no longer doubt that it will be fulfilled.

Humanity will learn to anchor itself in this universal, eternal space. It knows that the power of constant recreation and transformation occurs through this anchoring. And by seeing this so clearly in front of you, suddenly liberated from the hypnosis of banishment, a mighty vow grows within you: You will do everything to make this field spread more rapidly. Wherever you can, you will help end suffering. You will take responsibility for your life, for your immediate surroundings and beyond. You will take an active interest in the destiny of others and help us to awaken together to who we truly are.

CHAPTER 3: LIBERATED EROS AND ITS REALIZATION

SEXUALITY AND VIOLENCE

#MeToo![4] Who among us women could not describe situations in which we were sexually harassed or ran through dark alleys in a large city beset by fear, or felt threatened by men staring at us lewdly. Many secret rapes and sexual abuses would never have come to light without the #MeToo debate. That is its great merit.

We live in a world in which millions and millions of women are victims of sexual violence; the United Nations even speaks of a billion. Mass rape is used as a strategic weapon in all wars. But not only men are the perpetrators of sexual violence: The indescribable injuries through female genital mutilation – which occurs 6000 times a day – are perpetrated mostly by women. The suffering of the victims of sexual violence is so hopeless and immeasurable that an ocean of tears wells up, as well as a cry of indignation!

How can we end sexual violence worldwide, in every country, every culture, every family and every work relationship? We must raise our voices – powerfully and decisively. We must give women the courage so they dare to speak truthfully about what they have experienced. But we must especially understand the reasons for it. How was it even possible for an entire culture and society to develop in which this kind of violent crime became an everyday occurrence?

I could also cry out: Me too! I, too, am a victim of a failed sexual development. However, I am not accusing individual perpetrators but a wrongly organized system of love in which truth and beauty between the sexes could not live.

---

[4] About #MeToo: The revolt by actresses against sexual abuse in Hollywood in the autumn of 2017 triggered a worldwide debate – #MeToo – about sexual power and violence – not only in the film industry.

The debate about sexual abuse shows us the failed structures of a globalized society in which, 50 years after our so-called sexual liberation, there are no protected spaces of trust and truth. It shows, in a blatantly obvious way, that in a society based on the capitalist laws of profit and power, the erotic attraction between the sexes had to lose its whole and sacred core. It shows us that, within this system of life, we are not able to arrange our sexual reality so that it unfolds its healing power. A sexuality that is characterized by trust and contact will never lead to violence. But if the healing sexual reality in a society cannot unfold freely, and the magic and the power of attraction is not honored and celebrated but suppressed and concealed, the result is a social underground that nobody can understand. Crime, antagonism, perversion and torture are prevalent in the forbidden niches of society until they come to the surface with stupendous power in wars and crisis situations. They then tear everything down with them and nobody can stand up to their anonymous power.

#MeToo is an outcry of the sexes showing that we all find ourselves in a dead end street. Do we have the knowledge and the courage to live in such a way that the erotic attraction between the sexes regains its dignity, truth and beauty – its healing power and sacredness?

In our modern world, people come together from different cultures. This leads to frequent misunderstanding and irritations in the erotic realm. Imagine if there were more experienced and knowing men and women who were sensitive and courageous enough to speak openly about these topics. A few individuals are already doing this. These are essential contributions to the transition to a free and multicultural society. This is about sexual knowledge that lets us understand what turns men as well as women into violent perpetrators; and it is about empowering women to no longer keep silent out of fear of men. For it is now essentially up to us women if a new humanism can become reality or not.

In this regard we – women and men – are challenged to create a movement of solidarity that understands our sexual background and is courageous enough to call a spade a spade. It is not about new enmities or a further hardening of the fronts between women and men, but about education that can lead to a deeper understanding and the end of sexual violence on Earth.

Awakening from Hypnosis

A great awakening is occurring in us women. The call for equal rights was only the beginning; truly leaving patriarchy is a much deeper issue. We can see the excessive suffering that has resulted from a history gone wrong. We see the struggle between victims and perpetrators that resulted from a great hypnosis. We realize that we can only awaken from this hypnosis if we no longer accuse men. Both men and women are victims of a failed history, and we are all accomplices. We no longer have anything to reproach ourselves for. A new solidarity is awakening.

Man has for a long time been able to live from his artificial strength. He is now beginning to understand what he has done to women and to life on Earth and how he thereby has robbed himself of his own happiness. He realizes that up to now he was not able to love a woman. He must realize that it was fear that hid beneath the mantle of power – fear disguised as imperiousness, rage and violence. He feels deep remorse, but also the knowledge that there can be forgiveness. Man begins to realize that woman is more than a tempting female – that she has a soul, a mind, her own knowledge and her own will. He begins to understand her history, her fate, her pain and his joint responsibility for it. Empathy opens his heart. Now that he is rediscovering his love of woman and opens up to her down to his core, the power game of the patriarchal world falls apart and he begins to seek her as a true partner.

We – man and woman – realize that we have ended up in a dead end street together; our challenge is to find a way out. An ocean of tears now carries with it what has so far separated us from the reality of life. By fully allowing these tears to flow, we are led to a powerful point of forgiveness. It is forgiveness that leads to the new state of presence we need. Together, we can use our power and love for life on Earth.

SEX AND THE SACRED

Sexuality is a powerful source for receiving and procreating life. In sexuality we arrive at the primal source of Creation. Sexuality is the deepest experience of union in the flesh. The animal within you is allowed! And it is not in conflict with the great mental and divine soul that is also you.

The miracle of sexuality does not only take place when living beings are conceived. Every reality emerges from such a miracle. The sky touching the earth is a profoundly sensual process. To the extent that humanity banished sexuality from the sacred, it cruelly disfigured its own essence. To the extent that animal nature was vilified, war could assert itself on Earth.

In many early cultures, animal nature was worshiped as a divine power. What we regard as primitive turns out to be future-oriented. If the animal within us is suppressed for too long, it becomes cruel. Then something always remains imprisoned in the dungeons of our subconscious and breaks loose as soon as our moral systems become fragile. Only when our animal nature is again fully accepted as a divine power can the soul be liberated and pacified and its longing find fulfillment.

Here, we should pause a while and fully absorb the message in these words. If consummated in full trust, sexuality leads us to our divine source. Here our most sacred source reveals itself to us. If we allow this thought, a different presence, a mystery, enters our life. An endless power of love flows from its experience, as does an equally endless power of healing. If we again allow the healing powers of life to flow within us, the act of making love moves to the center of our culture. This awareness gives rise to new archetypes – and a new kind of art.

How does the male and the female come together in the sacred space? For this, new icons want to emerge that are characterized by mutual devotion and respect and will awaken new trust in us and in future generations. Artists, poets and authors of the world, unite to create these new icons!

The Connection between Eros and Agape

There are impressive women, role models, who have steadfastly pursued the path of inner peace and thereby achieved great things. Hildegard von Bingen, Rosa Luxemburg, Etty Hillesum, the "Mother" of Auroville, Mother Teresa, Ruth Pfau and many others. Peace Pilgrim, the North-American woman who left her previous name and life and walked for peace for over 20 years, was gripped by a deep joy that never left her. She no longer had to work to find peace, for she had found peace within herself. She no longer had to go through confusing emotions or submit to constant practices to become a good person, because deep down she had made a decision.

Yet none of these women could unite Eros and Agape. The opposing forces remained within a deep subconscious layer of the soul. You either follow the path of neighborly love and renounce erotic fulfillment and the power of the source, or else you follow erotic longing – but then you come into conflict with envy and jealousy and with your desire to help and serve.

But my female longing is seeking the path of combining neighborly love with an erotic existence. There, an image of the soul is waiting for its fulfillment – the awakening woman, free of contempt and humiliation, and she is saying: I am thoroughly of a sexual nature and I am glad to be so. Not only during the sexual act, but in my whole life – in the way I participate in the fate of the world and in the way I give myself to those who need my help; in my love of the community; in my love relationships; in the flirt with the neighbor; as well as in my elementary contact with nature and in my loving care of all beings. Both the wild Lilith and Eve, the archetypal mother, live in me and are no longer opposites. Because I can again be who I am in my essence, my fixation on the man and my neediness towards him is resolved. I have for too long sought the fulfillment of all my longings – including my religious longing for contact with the universe and my longing for knowledge and a meaningful task – exclusively in man.

Now that the female is again respected in a culture of partnership, my deepest primal source as a woman opens up anew. Woman is free again. Eros does not only live in marriages and behind closed doors, but openly. She can reveal Eros in the way she talks, the way she dances, the way she moves and the way she dresses. She no longer has to hide it from the lecherous eyes of men and the lurking dangers of possible rapists. Her ideals of beauty are no longer dictated by the fashion industry or the tyranny of male ideas about alienated sexuality. Beauty is the fearless self-revelation of her essential nature.

She knows that this power is allowed. She knows that men, too, see, love, respect, affirm and need her. No longer does a woman have to fear not "getting" anyone in the erotic competition. She no longer has to get anyone. There are many ways to fulfill her desire for happiness in life, intimacy and Eros. The way of personal partnership is one of them. Our protection lies in a culture in which Eros is sacred, respected and celebrated again. This opens the door to an erotic peace culture based on trust.

The male world is looking for new archetypes, too. For too long now, men have been raised based on the model of the lone hero, which separated them from their true nature. What does true male strength look like? What do I love in a man?

The erotic presence, sex – yes, that too, but not only. I also love active empathy, a compassionate heart, social responsibility, creative impulses and an alert mind. A powerful image of a sensual Messiah keeps appearing in my heart. A nonviolent warrior, who knows and loves Eros and protects life and the community – not by fighting, but through soft power. A Christ who truly resurrects – sensual, loving, compassionate, communicative, active. A loving father who does not allow his son to go to war or that his daughter has to submit to patriarchal expectations.

Combining the male source with the female source is the task of our time. If we succeed with this step, we will birth a new culture of peace. It is a culture of love: Love does not want to rule over anyone,

but its power is greater than all violence. There will be no losers in
this new culture.

Women's Power

Hidden behind our female powerlessness there is a potentially great soft power. If we discover it, we can turn the wheel of history in a healing direction and truly end violence. For this we need basic sexual knowledge that comes from compassion with the fate of millions of women and children, and men as well.

I was so touched by the stories of some women who worked to help refugees on the island of Lesbos and let men cry for hours in their arms, or listened for nights on end as mistreated women told them of their stories. They experienced that compassion with the fate of a person is the first step towards healing. We could help so many refugees if fear no longer blocked our compassion!

One key for this is solidarity among women. If we can end the competition between women and the silence about our inner reality, we will have created the foundation for a new and true solidarity among women. Mature women can show young women much about the sexual and spiritual power that women have and how we can learn to use it consciously and compassionately.

This also means knowing our own sexual power and taking a stand for it. If we hide our desire, we will always only see ourselves as victims. But this suppression turns us into accomplices of the system that created this immense sexual despair and obsession to begin with. If we recognize this, we have a powerful lever in our hands to effect change. We can then resolve the demonic connection between victim and perpetrator ever more deeply, and will thereby take a new position that our culture has been anticipating for so long. Together, we can create social structures in which children and youths can grow up without fear and where trust and love between the genders can again become possible.

To acquire this sexual knowledge, we need women who stand up for their own sexual truth, whether it has been fulfilled or not. The issue never ends. Women over 40, women over 50, women over 60 –

every decade brings its own new discoveries. May a women's movement arise that goes beyond accusations and leads to a stream of solidarity among us women – and to a new love of men.

No woman should be punished for following her desire; no body should be mistreated; no sexual energy should be deflected towards violence; and no person or animal should be tortured. Instead, we want to celebrate our erotic beauty and dignity and the fact that we are physical beings.

Tens of thousands of women marched for peace in the streets of Israel and Palestine, and millions marched against the politics of Donald Trump in the United States. The dancing women's movement "One Billion Rising" against sexual violence triggered a great wave of attention and female self-confidence in all countries. This is how a revolution of sensual love could occur for all life and for the freedom and love between all living beings. Let us enter the dance for love, for our earth and our waters, and for the sensuality and protection of all life.

Twelve Theses for a New Women's Movement

If women reflect on their power of compassion with all beings, their love and their knowledge; if they no longer fight men, but also do not imitate them; and if they find deep solidarity and cooperation with each other, then a powerful, global women's power can arise. The following theses are suggestions for the coming together of women across all cultures and worldviews.

1. Overcoming patriarchy positively

Women's power is not directed against men and not against our love of men, but it decidedly leaves behind those male structures that have contributed to the worldwide destruction of life and love. The present desolate state of the planet could only occur because we women participated in and tolerated it. We have used our capacity for patience in the wrong place. Women's active support of patriarchy had to do and still has to do with their withdrawal and permanent silence. It was, however, forced on them by the worst possible means of torture and persecution. Nobody will find the way out of this dead end street without women taking a stand publicly. It is now up to us women to take political and sexual responsibility – something that has been missing for so long. We invite all committed men to cooperate with us in our work for peace.

2. Solidarity among women

Solidarity among women is the foundation for a new women's movement and a nonviolent culture. This must be a solidarity that will not falter if two women love the same man or the same woman. In addition to building our varied love relationships, we cultivate contact and community among women. Rivalry among us will cease because we no longer love privately and do not want to have a man all to ourselves. This way of thinking is not a part of the female nature; it has been forced upon us throughout history by vows of faithfulness and man's claim of ownership. We accepted it and gave up our own natural way of thinking and acting. Women who are determined to create a new female culture are coming together in the new, emerging women's field. We will fundamentally follow a policy of love and ensure that it spreads. We will take care of our friendships and our common interests through our participation in the issues of the world.

3. The sexual nature of woman

Woman will affirm her sexual nature and take responsibility for it. She will reconnect with the sexual paradise of the body from which the patriarchal god banished her. This patriarchal god was invented as the oppressor of woman and sexuality. Her true emancipation and her special dignity as a woman begins when she forms her sexual impulses consciously and integrates them socially. To unfold properly, sexuality requires truth and trust. Woman knows this: she can gently help men free themselves from their secret fears of impotence. An essential root cause for violence in society lies in a suppressed and misdirected sexuality. Women will no longer leave the solution of this issue up to men.

4. Love and faithfulness

Love cannot be fenced in. Love is not a private matter. The new woman knows this. You can only be faithful if you are allowed to love others, too. Faithfulness does not prove itself by excluding others but by including them. This is a natural principle of a new feminine ethic. Jealousy is not a part of love but belongs to a sick system of fear of abandonment and distrust. To realize free love and permanent faithfulness we need communities in which truth, transparency and trust can develop. Love is freed of fear, of restriction, of clinging and false vows of faithfulness through trust. Faithfulness arises when we decide to be faithful to what we love and publicly commit to it. If a woman is in the state of love, she can never be abandoned.

5. Partnership

Partnership is a high and seldomly reached goal in human evolution. It constitutes the highest level in the development of freely loving people. This is true for the cohabitation and collaboration between the genders and between any two human beings on this planet. Partnership is based on the principles of complementation and polarity as opposed to dominance and artificial equality. It is based on the principle of freedom as opposed to clinging. Partnership is based on the self-responsibility of both partners. It can only develop and exist in a spiritual field of love that is no longer tied to any conditions. Partnership therefore requires the emancipation of both genders.

6. Professions

Women will no longer leave the so-called male professions to men alone. They will incorporate feminine qualities and ways of thinking into all fields of research. These are especially the qualities of soft power and of gently dissolving resistances, of communication instead of disconnection and integration instead of collision. Women will integrate these qualities not only in the social realm but also in the political, technological and scientific fields. Technology and science are also in need of alternative ways of thinking in order to learn to deal with resistance and contradiction in a new way. A nonviolent culture begins with nonviolent thinking.

7. Networks of peace

The hearts of committed women dedicate themselves to overcoming all "isms" and dogmas, for they have always ultimately served to suppress the truths of life and repress sexuality. Women will follow the principles of openness and compassion. Their natural sensuality helps overcome the limitations of fear and the resulting violence. They participate actively in the development of an international ring of peace: a network of the heart beyond all religions, worldviews and political affiliations. Female power is the peace-creating force of soft power. It is no longer the power to destroy life, but to birth, care for and protect life worldwide.

8. Animals

There is feminine knowledge about the connectedness of all living beings. Women will reconnect with their instinct for protection, care and warmth for all things alive. They will free this ability from all sentimentality and decidedly confront the current reality of slaughterhouses, fur farms and animal laboratories. There can be no tolerance of the existing killer institutions of the patriarchal society. Everything in evolution that has eyes wants to live, see, recognize and participate in the wonder of Creation. Eyes are there to satisfy curiosity. It is cruel to kill young beings who are still at the beginning of their search for knowledge, in such a cold and distanced way, just to eat them. A new women's movement will also help end this madness. There is only one existence and what we do unto other creatures we also do unto ourselves. This is deeply ingrained in women's knowledge, both new and old. In a new women's movement, we will use all our mental, spiritual and sexual powers to end this massacre of our fellow creatures.

9. Ecology

Ecology is the teaching of the contact and co-existence of all living beings. The human being has disrupted this co-existence and has the task of healing it again. We are all organs of one existence. All living things are animated parts of the great family of Creation – Gaia, Earth. In this alliance of life, there are no enemies and no pests. As ecologists of a new culture, we do not only speak about living beings, we speak with them. The affirmation of our own wild nature opens us up to contact with outer nature and enables us to empathize, communicate and heal. "In cooperation with nature" is not a slogan but a real source of infinite knowledge, friendship and the soul quality of life. Water, energy and food are freely available for humanity if we follow the logic of nature. We thus become a conscious part of a living Earth that provides all beings with what they need to live. We again recognize human rights and Earth rights as one. This gives rise to an ethical consciousness that is guided by the basic values of life.

10. Religion

Women will connect with the original impulse of the religions of Creation in a new way. We thereby do not follow any dogma, catechism or church teachings. But there is a primal religious impulse that we love because it is a part of life. We do not have a religion with God at the top. Our religion is life itself. We cultivate the sacred quality of the world by being attentive to the simplest things and the secret that they hold. There are areas of awareness in life that cannot be defined or discussed. Women will actively access new archetypal forces in Creation that have healing powers for the soul.

11. Integrating rage

If we look back at this millennia-old masculine culture and see that the same insanity is going on today – insanity in love, insanity in technology, insanity in interactions with children and animals, insanity in war – we realize the necessity of an inner about-face. We can no longer be silent. It is too much. Too much blood has been spilled and is still being spilled. But we cannot simply give our anger free reign over this, for then even more blood would flow. We must transform our rage into an energy that doesn't stop at any resistance and does not let itself be intimidated by anything in the world. It is a quiet, mighty, very determined energy. Every revolution has so far given rise to new oppression. Now we will use our revolutionary power to end sexual violence and to end all suffering that the human being, especially men – with our acquiescence and complicity – have perpetrated so cruelly on all living beings. No longer against something, but with determination for something. We need the power of rage; not as a force against men, but as a force for the uncompromising protection of all life.

12. Soft power

Male domination has characterized more than 3000 years of history and has thereby created the principle of hard power. The power of male societies consisted of breaking resistances. This manifested itself in wars of conquest, wars of religion, methods of parenting and the technologies used when dealing with nature. These methods have taken man himself into a dead end street from which there is no way out without female help. We do not want to recreate the old matriarchal structures and we do not want to dominate or patronize men.

Soft power is the power to overcome resistance through the power of the heart – to conquer difficulties through ease. For this we either need thousands of years of training in Zen Buddhism – or else we use the powers that we women have naturally. Soft power is a regulating principle that even the most hardened men will submit to in the long run when they notice that it does not involve revenge, punishment or a hidden agenda; hardened men became so hardened because this soft power was missing. It is the power of mothers determined to protect their children. Soft power is a principle of evolution that takes hold immediately, once the principle of trust prevails.

THE GLOBAL LOVE SCHOOL

In addition to the continuous internal love school for the community at Tamera, in 2013 we established the Global Love School, which I and Benjamin von Mendelssohn are heading, supported by a team of experienced men and women from Tamera. The Global Love School has set itself the goal of developing humane and universal answers to the pressing questions in the area of love and sexuality. It is a question of developing consciousness in love and knowledge about how violence and suppression can end worldwide. The participants of the annually held ten-day, in-depth seminar are people who work worldwide in crisis areas as peace workers, activists, founders of communities, as well as journalists and social studies teachers, and who are confronted with unsolved issues of love and sexuality within their work.

To illustrate the work of the Love School, I quote from the report by one of our group leaders: "In a Forum, a man who works as an aid worker in the Congo goes into the middle of the circle. When he speaks of the fate of a 13-year-old girl, nobody can hold back their tears of compassion. It is a story of suffering with abuse in every conceivable form. In the course of his presentation, he reveals that he has discovered that the 'monster' perpetrator lives in him, too, and that it is a part of his male despair. This monster is the man who, because his love for his mother or her love for him could never be lived, wants to dominate women and avoid and destroy their source. In him, sexual fantasies are almost always connected to violence. This is true of almost all men of our times. And yet he loves and adores women more than anything else. He, who has dedicated his life to help the world, to help human beings, cannot live in this conflict. He seeks help and forgiveness and he seeks the rebirth within himself of the healthy man, who does not have to be ashamed of his fantasies and can be sure that there are women who will support him on this path." Whenever I speak about sexuality in public, I feel connected with such questions and fates. The global population needs new information in the areas of love and sexuality. Personal work with oneself, the active participation in global issues and the creation of new cultural models are inseparably connected with each other. We are thereby touching a taboo that is still being upheld in public discourse: the idea that love and sexuality are private issues that, at the most, are discussed with therapists.

The Global Love School has set itself the goal of establishing a new global consciousness regarding love, trust and truth between the sexes. Today, we are experiencing a wave of destruction of old social structures, including marriage. We need new forms of living together in community in which the intimate couple relationship is embedded, so that what was valuable in marriage and family is retained. The Global Love School wants to train leaders to become standard bearers for such communities.

Manifesto of the Global Love School

- There can be no peace on Earth as long as there is war in love.

- Love and sexuality are political issues. We no longer close our eyes to this fact.

- Love is more than a feeling; it requires social containers in which it can be lived and realized. It requires an ethic in which we can become truthful.

- Independent of what our personal lives may look like right now – if we live alone or in community, if we are celibate or married, monogamous or polygamous – we are working together to develop a perspective for our children and the generations that come after us.

- We are seeking answers in the area of love so that our children can trust us again and find a true home. We are seeking answers that awaken pleasure and curiosity within us and others, and that are stronger than the fear of again being hurt when dealing with the hot topics in love.

- Free sexuality and partnership do not exclude each other; on the contrary, they complement each other. Truth in love is the foundation for every permanent love relationship. The question of whether we want to be monogamous or polygamous, heterosexual or homosexual, is determined based on our inner truth

- Longing for a partner and at the same time longing for erotic adventures is not cheating. It only becomes cheating if we keep it a secret from our partners.

- There is a faithfulness in which the attraction of one of the love partners to a third person no longer elicits a fear of abandonment in us, but instead joy and an increase in Eros and trust. One day we will wake up with this experience and say: Our adventure is no longer in war but in love. Eros has become our sacred source of life and love.

- We anchor sexuality in the universal order of life again. It is sacred to us – just as sacred as life itself.

- The connection between Eros and religion gives rise to an erotic culture in which war becomes unthinkable. We see the chance to end the war in love and thus to initiate entirely new forms of living together and new social structures. Love is the most important germinal force for a new peace culture – a culture not built on abstention but on the affirmation of the fullness of life.

- Here, there is a way out of the dead end street of our times that is becoming increasingly visible, towards a culture of partnership between man and woman. No mother will send her sons off to war again. No father will have to give his life to protect his country again.

- There will no longer be a war industry or ministries of defense. The military bases will be turned into peace universities, in which the protection of this planet can be practiced and learned.

- Love and sexuality are basic topics for every awakening person who wishes to become a responsible member of this culture.

- A new global network of lovers and gardeners of a new Earth will emerge – Terra Nova – in which Eros and permanence in love have a chance to blossom again.

For the future of all children.

FINAL NOTE: A BIRTHDAY PARTY

Meanwhile, we are looking back at 40 years of project history. The community has grown enormously. The children who have been born here are now part of the generation of leaders. There is a worldwide network of cooperating partners and groups who also wish to establish Healing Biotopes and to use Tamera as a training center.

Many people say that coming to Tamera is like arriving at a new planet. I would like to describe it based on my daughter Vera's birthday party. Using the socially traditional concepts, one could say: The parents, in-laws and step-parents gathered around the birthday girl with their former and current spouses. New partners and ex-partners, their children and half siblings, and also occasional lovers, celebrate her birthday in harmony and friendship; they flirt and openly show their attraction and love for each other. In this network of love, new love affairs do not give rise to separation but to deepened friendship. People, who without the support of the community would have become archenemies, now celebrate together in intimate friendship and joy.

This is not only true for a party; they also live and work together; their children grow up together; and, of course, a woman occasionally takes care of the child of her partner's lover when the two want to spend intimate time together. If allowed, a liberated Eros can lead to entirely new "tribal constellations." The endless dramas or hypocritical indignation that can be found in soap operas here becomes

the foundation for living together in an emotionally safe way, in solidarity with each other.

It is wonderful for children to be able to grow up in such an environment. They have playmates of all ages; they can explore the world, ask about anything and feel safe everywhere. In addition to their permanent home with their parents, they have other adults they relate to, whom they trust and who can show them exciting things, as well as older children and youths who are role models for them.

When Vera's young son was a year and a half old, he knew the first names of practically everyone in the community.

Meanwhile, four generations live together in Tamera. More and more permanent love relationships are formed, for free love no longer conjures up fear. All this would not have been possible without work and without confronting old fears. By working decisively on ourselves, committed to remaining faithful to truth and trust, and using our minds for a new way of thinking, we have made the exhilarating discovery that a free Eros enriches our relationships instead of destroying them.

APPENDIX

The kiss, 2013
Photo: Ludwig Schramm

An Epilogue by Leila Dregger

A Free Love Couple, A Partnership in Service to the World

When I got to know Project Meiga, I heard a statement that truly inspired me: Every act of making love is a service to the world. Over the course of the years it became clear to me, mainly through the example of the authors of this book, that this statement is not limited to sexual encounters, but refers to love overall. A partnership between a man and a woman – with their polar opposites, the inevitable conflicts and the solidarity in resolving them – serves the world deeper than anything else.

Sabine Lichtenfels and Dieter Duhm have been a couple within the framework of free love for over 40 years. And they are more: They are partners in building a project that has been working to create a model of a peace culture. A great network has been created around their partnership, which includes communities and peace initiatives as well as ecological, spiritual and social research projects. Through their example and their assistance, hundreds, even thousands of people have been inspired to seek alternatives to the capitalist system, question their path in love, and commit themselves to more truth and trust. Through them innumerable people have opened their eyes to the fact that a different world, a different life, is not only possible, but already exists.

When they first met, one would not have suspected that such a productive partnership would come about. Their approaches were too different.

He – born at the end of World War II – was a refugee child, became active in the church as a youth, did his military service as a pacifist and accompanied all stations in his life with painting. Alarmed by the Vietnam War and other crimes of western societies, he became one of the leading figures in the student movement and wrote the bestseller Angst im Kapitalismus [Fear in Capitalism]. Having been offered three professorships, which he declined, he went into retreat for half a year in a farmhouse in Lower Bavaria to ponder how to continue his life. When he met Sabine Lichtenfels, he was not looking for a love relationship; he was looking for partners to establish a new social model.

She, having grown up in a solid, middle-class family of musicians, was "always in love, for as long as I could remember," and sneaked out at night from her parents' house, full of curiosity about sensuality and Eros. She became politically active at a young age. Early on, she also discovered her psychic talents and her intimate relationship with the core of all beings and things. Her source was, and is, the oneness with All That Is, a very earthy and physical spirituality and the power of the heart that lies in connection. She was the thinking heart of her circle of friends and, at the age of 16, she decided to establish a village where lovers never again had to leave each other. She studied theology, not out of piety, but out of a love of Jesus, the revolutionary. She got married and gave birth to a child, but could not appease her husband's chronic jealousy. She finally realized that this narrow form of life without community kills love.

Their first encounters and their beginning friendship were full of enthusiasm and dedication to a joint vision. Their awakening love consisted mainly of a sensual joy of discovery and amazement at their polarity. "What? That's how a woman thinks?" and "That's what a man feels?" were questions that were more interesting to them than any vows of faithfulness or romantic ideas about the future. Although they were enthusiastic about their common goal, they represented totally different approaches. They were, as they realized, thoroughly polar forces – man and woman.

They realized that there was more to their deepening partnership than their private happiness. They discovered the possibility of resolving the difficulties between the genders in an exemplary way and therefore decided not to hide or placate their conflicts and differences, but to take them on as tasks.

This was a courageous decision, for as all people from our culture, they also come from a patriarchal culture that has produced a deep war between the genders. The injuries in the relationship between man and woman are so deep that this collective trauma intrudes into every partnership with such a force that most people shy away from even touching it. In almost all relationships, this issue is either suppressed or else there is a divorce. The two authors of this book decided to contribute, through their own personal example, to healing this deepest wound of humanity. The conflicts between man and woman are one of the global issues that require healing – by people who have enough courage and knowledge to do so.

They knew they had to create a human environment for this: a community that could engender solidarity, truth, trust and intimacy in its participants; a community interested in researching what was behind the points of pain and sudden sensitivities and willing to accompany them with warm-hearted solidarity; a community that provided social embeddedness with a joint clear ethical approach to truth, trust and solidarity.

They openly revealed relationship conflicts that every couple knows but are normally kept secret. This often happened clearly outside of their comfort zone, but the resulting cognitive process was enormous for everyone. There is probably no other couple that has addressed and dealt with their difficulties in such a sincere, supportive and discerning way. At the same time, I know of no other cultural approach that unites such polar forces: feeling and thinking, science and faith, theory and practice. If polarity is allowed, a new culture and an exciting life ensues. This is one of the great gifts from the founders' partnership.

This first joint book was written based on these experiences, this struggle, these insights and this cooperation. Dieter Duhm recently said: "When men begin to believe women, patriarchy has ended." The opposite is also true.

May this book contribute to more and more women and men truly believing each other and working together for a future without war, for a love and sexuality without lies and violence.

Further Information

Whoever wants to delve deeper into the thoughts presented in this book and wishes to help implement them is very welcome to do so. Please contact us. It is in the interest of all to end sexual violence on Earth as soon as possible. For this, the global "Healing Biotopes Plan" was created, which we wish to realize.

We ask you to support this work using every effort and every means at your disposal. Please help disseminate this book. Organize events about the contents presented here and arrange artistic activities to ensure that these topics are discussed. We gladly welcome constructive suggestions and offer support wherever needed.

We invite all those interested to use the weekly Ring of Power meditation that Sabine Lichtenfels has initiated to connect, together with others, with the source of power. More information on her webpage: www.sabine-lichtenfels.com.

We are also grateful for every financial donation. We will use them to disseminate the contents of this book.

Verlag Meiga c/o Tamera
Monte do Cerro • 7630-392 Relíquias • Portugal
Ph: +351 283 635 344 • E-Mail: info@verlag-meiga.org
www.verlag-meiga.org

Donation Account
Account holder: Grace-Stiftung zur Humanisierung des Geldes
Bank: Raiffeisenbank Zürich ((The bank's post check account number: 87-71996-7) Clearing 81487

Transfers in Euro:	in CHF:
Account No.: 92188.69	92188.56
IBAN: CH9881487000009218869	CH6181487000009218856
BIC: RAIFCH22	RAIFCH22

Bibliography

Abrams, Douglas: The Lost Diary of Don Juan. Washington Square Press.

Caddy, Peter: In Perfect Timing. Findhorn Press.

de Chardin, Teilhard Pierre: The Phenomenon of Man. Harper Perennial.

Deschner, Karlheinz: Das Kreuz mit der Kirche. Econ.

Duhm, Dieter: Eros Unredeemed. The World Power of Sexuality. Verlag Meiga.

Duhm, Dieter: The Sacred Matrix. From the Matrix of Violence to the Matrix of Life. Verlag Meiga.

Duhm, Dieter: Terra Nova. Global Revolution and the Healing of Love. Verlag Meiga.

Dregger, Leila: Tamera. A Model for the Future. Verlag Meiga.

Eisler, Riane: The Chalice and the Blade. HarperSanFrancisco.

Emmermann, Heidemarie: Credo an Gott und sein Fleisch (Hoffmann & Campe)

Estés, Clarissa: Women Who Run with the Wolves. Ballantine Books.

Geusen, Madjana: Man's Holy Grail is Woman. Paintings, Drawings and Texts by Dieter Duhm. Verlag Meiga.

Jong, Erica: Fear of Flying. Penguin Books.

Lichtenfels, Sabine: Grace. Pilgrimage for a Future without War. Verlag Meiga.

Lichtenfels, Sabine: Sources of Love and Peace. Morning Prayers. Verlag Meiga.

Lichtenfels, Sabine: Temple of Love. Journey into the Age of Sensual Fulfillment. Verlag Meiga.

Lichtenfels, Sabine: Traumsteine. Reise in das Zeitalter der sinnlichen Erfüllung. Hugendubel

Lichtenfels, Sabine: Weiche Macht. Perspektiven eines neuen Frauenbewusstseins und einer neuen Liebe zu den Männern. Verlag Meiga.

Long, Barry: Making Love: Making Love the Divine Way. Barry Long Books.

Lusseyran, Jacques: And There Was Light: Autobiography of Jacques Lusseyran: Blind Hero of the French Resistance. Morning Light Press.

Miller, Alice: Breaking Down the Wall of Silence: The Liberating Experience of Facing Painful Truth. Basic Books.

Neumann, Erich: The Great Mother: An Analysis of the Archetype. Princeton University Press.

Peace Pilgrim: Her Life and Work in Her Own Words. Ocean Tree Books.

Reich, Wilhelm: The Murder of Christ: The Emotional Plague of Mankind. Farrar, Straus and Giroux.

Schubart, Walter: Religion und Eros. Beck.

Villon, François: Die lasterhaften Balladen und Lieder des François Villon. Nachdichtung von Paul Zech (dtv)

Winiecki, Martin (Ed.): Setting Foundations for a New Civilization. Perspectives for the Global Revolution. Study materials from the Terra Nova School. Verlag Meiga.

Ywahoo, Dhyani: Voices of Our Ancestors: Cherokee Teachings from the Wisdom Fire. Shambhala Publications, Inc.

PICTURES OF THE AUTHORS

Dr. Dieter Duhm

born in 1942 in Berlin, is an art historian and psychoanalyst with a doctorate in sociology. In 1967, as an activist in the German students' movement, he combined the idea of political revolution with that of individual liberation and became known through his book Angst im Kapitalismus [Fear in Capitalism]. In 1978 he founded the "Bauhütte" project, out of which the Healing Biotopes project emerged, first in Germany and, since 1995, in Portugal under the name Tamera, a center for concrete utopia and international peace work. Today, he heads the Akron School there, a monastic-political training for young peace workers, as well as the departments of Eros, Art and Healing. **www.dieter-duhm.com**

In front of the painting by D. Duhm "Sunrise over the Walls of Chernobyl," 2018 – Photo: Delia Wöhlert

Sabine Lichtenfels

born in 1954, is a theologist, one of the "1000 Women for Peace," and a co-founder of Tamera. She is the founder of the Global Love School, head of spiritual research and patron of Terra Deva for the cooperation with elemental beings. She led and accompanied peace pilgrimages through Israel and Palestine (2005, 2007) and through Colombia (2008, 2010), California (2015) and Portugal (2009, 2016), along with several hundred participants. She initiated the Ring of Power, a political meditation network for peace workers from all parts of the world.

www.sabine-lichtenfels.com

Dieter Duhm (left), Sarah Vollmer (middle), Sabine Lichtenfels (right) with the newly created community, 1979

Teaching during the Love School, Tamera, 2017
Photo: Simon du Vinage

Painting nudes at the Oracle Source, Tamera, 2018
Photo: Naila von Mendelssohn

Addressing the peace village San José de Apartadó in Colombia, 2008
Photo: David Osthoff

Tibetan lamas blessing Sabine Lichtenfels in Tamera, 2008
Photo: Delia Wöhlert

Dieter Duhm with his daughter Mara, 1988

... and with his daughter Vera, 2017
Photo: Simon du Vinage

Sabine Lichtenfels with her grandson Leon, 2018
Photo: Dieter Duhm

For the Future of our Children, 2018
Photo: Delia Wöhlert

DIETER DUHM

TERRA NOVA: GLOBAL REVOLUTION AND THE HEALING OF
LOVE

Based on the experience of one of the most radical communitarian
experiments of our time, Dieter Duhm outlines a compelling vision
and pathway towards a new global culture – a society free of violence,
love free of fear, life based on trust and solidarity. Terra Nova offers
profound perspectives for all those looking for alternatives to our
current dominant culture.

In times when the world is full of wars and catastrophes, when resistance against the existing order soars and revolt is in the air, Dieter
Duhm publishes the draft for a humane future society. Terra Nova
is not a book for fast solutions and recipes; it relates to the existential questions of our times such as, "Is there still a realistic hope for
a future worth living?", "Will we survive the social and ecological
crises we have brought about?", "Will we make it?"

In his latest offering, the sociologist, psychoanalyst and co-founder
of the Tamera peace research center takes a profound view into the
roots of the global crisis, while at the same time pointing out foundations of planetary renewal, as they have become visible in decades
of research.

*"This magnificent visionary book proposes real practical
solutions for building a new world. Read it and inspire yourself.
Change the world!"*

Andrew Harvey
Institute for Sacred Activism, USA

VERLAG MEIGA

DIETER DUHM

TERRA NOVA
GLOBAL REVOLUTION
AND THE HEALING OF LOVE

Hardcover • 224 pages • 27 4-colored photos
ISBN 978-3-927266-54-4 • 17,80 Euro
E-Book: ISBN 978-3-927266-56-8 • 8,88 Euro

Lightning Source UK Ltd.
Milton Keynes UK
UKHW050317230120
357430UK00007B/27